Musical Mysteries

TRUE CRIME HISTORY SERIES

MYSTERIES

From Mozart

to

John Lennon

ALBERT BOROWITZ

The Kent State University Press

Kent, Ohio

© 2010 by The Kent State University Press, Kent, Ohio 44242
All rights reserved
Library of Congress Catalog Card Number 2009047059
ISBN 978-1-60635-026-3
Manufactured in the United States of America

"'Pore Jud is Daid': Violence and Lawlessness in the Plays of Lynn Riggs" and "La-mech, the Second Biblical Killer: A Song with Variations" were first published in *Legal Studies Forum*. "Lully and the Death of Cambert" and "Gilbert and Sullivan on Corporation Law: *Utopia, Limited* and the Panama Canal Frauds" first appeared in Albert Borowitz, *A Gallery of Sinister Perspectives: Ten Crimes and a Scandal* (Kent, Ohio: Kent State Univ. Press, 1982), and are reprinted here with permission. "The Stalking of John Lennon" first appeared as a chapter in Albert Borowitz, *Terrorism for Self-Glorification: The Herostratos Syndrome* (Kent, Ohio: Kent State Univ. Press, 2005), and is reprinted with permission.

Library of Congress Cataloging-in-Publication Data
Borowitz, Albert, 1930–
    Musical mysteries : from Mozart to John Lennon / Albert Borowitz.
        p.   cm. — (True crime history series)
    Includes index.
    ISBN 978-1-60635-026-3 (hbk. : alk. paper) ∞
    1. Music and crime. 2. Crime in music. 3. Musicians—Death. I. Title.
    ML3916.B6 2010
    780'.0364—dc22   2009047059

British Library Cataloging-in-Publication data are available.

14 13 12 11 10   5 4 3 2 1

In memory of

Jonathan Goodman,

generous friend

and

master of crime history

Contents

Preface

Since this volume is entitled *Musical Mysteries,* I should begin, as old-fashioned music used to do, by clearly announcing the principal themes. In my discussion (in Part One) of the encounters of musicians with homicide, real or suspected, I will be emphasizing three recurring motifs. The first will be envy and competition between musicians. The second theme will be in the form of a question: Can genius and criminality coexist in the same soul? And finally a third theme will keep cropping up like a rondo subject: the jarring contrast between the sublime activity of the creative artist and the violent melodrama of everyday life from which none of us—musicians included—is safe.

Let us begin with theme one, envious and competitive musicians. Who was the first of them to suffer the pangs of rivalry gone mad? If we were to urge the claim of Antonio Salieri to this sinister distinction, we would be many millennia too late. Perhaps the earliest example of a composer-performer who turned to murder to eliminate a competitor was the very inventor of the musical arts, the god Apollo. This well-known story has a Mozartian ring for it features the first magic flute, a double flute that Athena made from a stag's bones and played at a banquet of the gods. She was nettled to see that Hera and Aphrodite were laughing at her behind their hands while all the other gods seemed quite transported by the music. After the concert "she went away by herself into a Phrygian wood, took up the flute again beside a stream, and watched her image in the water, as she played." Immediately she understood why the two goddesses had laughed at her. Her efforts on the instrument had turned her face an unflattering blue and caused her cheeks to swell. In disgust "she threw down her flute, and laid a curse on anyone who picked it up."

The unfortunate victim of Athena's spell was the satyr Marsyas. No sooner did he put the flute to his lips than it played by itself, reproducing Athena's divine music. The satyr, though, claimed the music as his own and wandered through Phrygia enthralling the peasants with his performance. They told him that even Apollo couldn't do better on his lyre, and Marsyas was foolish enough to accept their critical appraisal. His vainglory provoked the anger of Apollo, who invited him to a music contest, "the winner of which should inflict whatever punishment he pleased on the loser." Marsyas consented, and Apollo impaneled the Muses as a jury—as clear a fix as there ever was at least before the judging scandals in modern Olympics. The Muses claimed to be charmed by both instruments until Apollo came up with a trick. He challenged Marsyas to do with the flute what the god could do with the lyre. Turn it upside down, he ordered, and both play and sing at the same time. Marsyas failed to meet this tall order, but Apollo, with ease, "reversed his lyre and sang . . . delightful hymns in honour of the Olympian gods." The Muses awarded victory to Apollo. Thereupon the god took cruel revenge on the musical upstart Marsyas. He flayed him alive and nailed his skin to a pine tree.

If the divine creator of music could be moved to murder by envy of a mortal competitor, how was more restrained behavior to be expected from Salieri and his ilk? My article, "Salieri and the 'Murder' of Mozart," published seven years before Peter Shaffer's *Amadeus,* explores not only the envy motif but also the psychological compatibility of genius and crime. A classic (but optimistic) pronouncement on the latter subject is attributable to Wolfgang Amadeus Mozart himself, not, however, as he appears in Shaffer's drama but in the pages of Alexander Pushkin's chamber play *Mozart and Salieri.* A seventeenth-century analogue to the whispering campaign against Salieri was the assertion that opera composer Jean-Baptiste Lully, after driving his rival Robert Cambert out of the French theaters, murdered him in England.

The claims that homicide caused the deaths of Mozart and Cambert are ungrounded, but the mysterious murder of eighteenth-century composer and violinist Jean-Marie Leclair is well documented by surviving records of the police investigation. The solution to the case that I propose on the basis of my examination of the detective work suggests that the killing of Leclair was inspired by envy and a sense of frustration over the failure of musical ambition.

The third theme of Part One of *Musical Mysteries* will show musicians trapped in lurid events of everyday life, in tales of homicide more suited to the *Police Gazette* than to the *Musical Quarterly*. In these true stories the musician appears as vengeful husband or as victim of a mistress's former lover. Perhaps the greatest musician to have figured as murderer in a domestic tragedy was the madrigal composer Carlo Gesualdo, Prince of Venosa. In 1586 he married a noble Neapolitan lady, Donna Maria d'Avalos. Four years later, having learned of her love affair with the Duke of Andria, he had her murdered by servants and himself took an active part in the killing. A century later another Italian composer, Alessandro Stradella, became as famous for amatory scandal and tragedy as for his music. After eloping with the mistress of a Venetian nobleman, Stradella was wounded by assassins sent from Venice. But he did not change his ways. Another group of avengers, apparently in punishment of a later romantic escapade, murdered Stradella in 1682.

Unlike the murders of Stradella and of Gesualdo's wife and her lover, which were actuated by passion and a desire for revenge, the violence of the modern age does not always derive from a personal link between assailant and victim. Killings committed at random or among persons unknown to each other are now common occurrences. *Musical Mysteries* recounts the deaths of three celebrated twentieth-century composers who died at the hands of complete or virtual strangers. In the evening of September 15, 1945, three shots fired in panic by a soldier in the American army of occupation in post–World War II Austria deprived the music world of one of its modernist geniuses, Anton Webern. My chapter on the composer's death summarizes evidence uncovered by Hans Moldenhauer regarding the circumstances of the tragedy and pursues echoes of the case in literature and in an Internet hoax. American composer Marc Blitzstein had made only the slightest acquaintance with the three sailors who attacked him in Fort-de-France, Martinique, on January 21, 1964. After coming upon Blitzstein at a waterfront bar and accompanying him on a pub crawl, they robbed and beat him in an alley. Blitzstein, who throughout his musical career had sung the praises of the common man, died in a hospital on the following evening. His plan for the night of the assault may have been a rough-trade sexual encounter, but the sailors were satisfied with the contents of his wallet. Mark David Chapman, the perpetual failure who stalked and killed the famous Beatle John Lennon, was also unknown to his victim. In his world of private fantasies, however, Chapman had more and more embedded himself in the name and personality of Lennon, whom he simultaneously admired and envied. Like the ancient Greek arsonist Herostratos, Chapman hoped to achieve fame through the destruction of his idol.

Part Two of this work, "Crime in Music," considers three examples, widely separated in time and culture, of the use of crime subjects in various musical forms and genres. In my study "Lamech, the Second Biblical Killer: A Song with Variations," the exploits of Cain's descendant, Lamech, are encapsulated in an enigmatic set piece that he sings for his two wives in Genesis. In the "Song of Lamech," or the "Song of the Sword," as his lyric outburst is called, he boasts of two killings that outdo fratricide. I trace variant interpretations of Lamech's song from Rabbinic commentaries to Victorian poetry. Lamech has attracted the attention of many English writers, including Chaucer, Kipling, George Eliot, and Arthur Clough; these authors have portrayed him as the first multiple murderer, the father of feuds, and an innovator in murder weaponry. He is also an early embodiment of inherited criminality.

George Bernard Shaw found the libretto of Gilbert and Sullivan's 1893 operetta *Utopia, Limited* completely puzzling. From a clue in promoter Goldbury's patter song, I develop the thesis that the plot was inspired by the Panama Canal criminal fraud case of the same year and relate the Goldbury song to Gilbert's career-long interest in law and crimes, whether perpetrated by businessmen, thieves, or murderers.

As my finale, I offer an elucidation of the character Jud Fry in Rodgers and Hammerstein's *Oklahoma!* I explore Jud's roots in Lynn Riggs's play *Green Grow the Lilacs,* on which *Oklahoma!* is based, and consider other works by Riggs that deal with violence and lawlessness. The study also draws on insights into Riggs's life (including a family murder and a fire) that were communicated to me in interviews with the playwright's then-surviving relatives.

What are the "mysteries" that my title promises? Some of my chapters offer genuine whodunnits. Who killed Leclair or Stradella? In other cases, the mystery runs deeper. Was a crime committed at all, or have Lully and Salieri been wrongly accused through all these centuries? In several instances that I study here, we never learn the roots of the violent act. Why did Lamech surpass Cain by taking the lives of two victims, and what was the motive of the sailors who attached Marc Blitzstein? Such questions are mysteries of the human soul, the most intractable enigmas of all.

Bibliographical Notes

The story of Apollo recounted here comes from Robert Graves, *The Greek Myths* (Baltimore: Penguin, 1955), 1:77.

Throughout the volume, the translations of foreign-language works are mine unless otherwise noted.

Part One

The Musician as Murderer
or Victim

1

Lully and the Death of Cambert

Musicians have not been immune to the venom of professional rivalry. Tradition appears to attribute the most intense rivalries to operatic composers. In the case of one of the great competitive pairings, Gluck and Piccinni, neither man seems to have had any basis to reproach the other for acts of unfairness. The guilty parties were the factions of the Paris opera world that attempted unsuccessfully to pit the two men against each other in an operatic mano a mano by assigning them the same libretto based on Quinault's *Roland*. The legends of other rivalries are darker. In the accounts of the enmity of Salieri for Mozart and of the victory of Jean-Baptiste Lully over Robert Cambert, we read not only testimonies to professional antagonism but also hints or outright charges of assassination.

The Mozart-Salieri traditions have often been summarized and will be the subject of detailed examination in the next chapter. However, the story of how Lully came to be blamed for the death of Cambert in London in 1677 is relatively little known to the English-reading public. In fact, little effort has been made by prior researchers (principally French) to determine whether the traditional view that Cambert died violently can be documented from English records. My two purposes here will be to review the anti-Lully traditions that have grown up around Cambert's death and to demonstrate, on the basis of a survey of English records, the difficulty of producing evidence that Cambert was murdered by anyone at all.

It is not an accident that the most extreme traditions of musical rivalry from the seventeenth and eighteenth centuries derive from the world of opera. Many factors fed the potentialities for conflict that are never

3

wholly lacking when sensitive artists are struggling to find acceptance for their work. Due to the cultural centralism of monarchic society and the great expense of opera productions, the commissioning and subsidizing of operas were primarily under control of the court. The success of opera composers was accordingly determined not only by talent but also by the political strength of their supporters. Courtiers electioneered for the opera composers under their patronage, and their campaigns were marred by "dirty tricks."

The passions stirred by opera politics were further inflamed by nationalism. In the seventeenth and eighteenth centuries, Italian opera, and Italian operatic composers and troupes, were exported to the major European capitals, where they met with native resistance. To the extent that this led to adaptation of Italian style or development of newer national styles, such resistance was musically fruitful, but it also took its toll in personal animosities directed against the cultural invaders. The libels against Salieri were based in large measure on his Italian origin. Lully was not able, either by his writ of naturalization from Louis XIV or the changed spelling of his name, to convince the people of Paris that he had, "in spite of all temptations to belong to other nations," become a true Frenchman.

The story of the competition of Cambert and Lully for mastery of the French opera world might read like the race of the hare and the tortoise if we were to attribute more cunning to the tortoise than is granted by proverb. Cambert was off the mark thirteen years sooner, but he rested for a decade; when success was in sight, his more resourceful adversary overtook him.

Cambert's musical career in Paris was anchored by significant official posts. He served as organist of the Church of St. Honoré and, from 1662 or 1663, as Anne of Austria's Master of Music. Early in his career Cambert conceived the idea of creating a *comédie en musique* in the French language. Under Cambert's concept, musical continuity would be provided by the use of recitative on the Italian model, and the singers would move freely about the stage instead of striking wooden postures. Cambert's first effort in the new operatic genre, written to a libretto by the clumsy and conceited poet Pierre Perrin, was the so-called *Pastorale of Issy*, which was performed at a private country home at Issy near Paris in 1659. Unfortunately, Cambert was never inclined or able to push the borders of opera beyond pastoral scenes. A second opera, *Ariane et Bacchus*, was composed in 1659 under a commission from Mazarin, but its performance was called off after Mazarin's death.

Cambert did not turn to opera again until 1669, when he renewed his association with Perrin, who in June of that year had obtained a royal *privilège* authorizing him to organize an *Académie de musique* for the production of opera. In March 1671 Cambert and Perrin presented their opera *Pomone* as the inaugural work of the Académie. It was immensely successful and may have enjoyed more than seventy performances within an eight-month period.

It is speculated that the success of *Pomone* encouraged Lully to enter the opera world and make it his own, to the exclusion of Cambert and other possible rivals. However, he might have arrived at the same destination in any event, though his route was circuitous. The narrative of the spectacular rise of Lully from obscurity is well-known. A son of an Italian miller, Lully was brought to Paris as a youth to serve Mademoiselle de Montpensier (la Grande Mademoiselle) as an Italian tutor and attendant. Having displayed musical precocity while in her employ, he was astute enough to change sides during the wars of the Fronde and to enter the service of the young Louis XIV. Enjoying Louis' admiration and affection, Lully began as dancer, ballet director, and orchestra conductor and then became an important court composer, both of ballets and ceremonials and of incidental music to the comedies of another favorite of Louis XIV, Molière. About the same time as the premiere of *Pomone*, Lully's *Psyche* was produced. Although ballet and stage machinery remained dominant, critics agree that elements of opera were also present in the work.

Somehow, Lully became convinced that he should acquire the Perrin privilège and fashion a wider musical monopoly for himself. It is not clear whether the idea originated in Lully's own ambition or in the encouragement of Colbert or Mme de Montespan or Louis XIV himself. Lully always attributed the idea to the king, and it would certainly have been consistent with the king's belief that each important task of the nation, whether political or cultural, should be exclusively committed to trusted hands.

In any event, Lully's original acquisition of the Perrin privilège cannot be regarded as a wrong to Cambert. The theater partnership that had been operating under the privilège had been torn by dissension, Perrin was languishing in debtors' prison, and Cambert's role in the venture had been reduced to that of a hired musician (hired but, alas, not paid). Lully worked out a businesslike agreement with Perrin for the transfer of the privilège in consideration for Lully's discharge of Perrin's debts. Lully's transgressions against his musical colleagues, including Cambert, arose

Portrait of Jean-Baptiste Lully, engraved by Jean-Louis Roullet.

not from his agreement with Perrin but from his ruthlessness in obtaining and enforcing a new royal privilège of unparalleled scope. Under this broad authority, and undeterred by litigation brought by his adversaries, Lully closed the theater at which *Pomone* had triumphed, raided its opera troupe, drove all competing opera composers from the field, and even placed severe restrictions on musical accompaniment in the theater of his old collaborator, Molière.

The musical career of Cambert in London has been traced, as well as the scanty records permit, by André Tessier and W. H. Grattan Flood in separate studies published in 1927 and 1928. Cambert arrived in London in either 1672 or 1673. He was possibly influenced to make this move by the fact that his student Louis Grabu was Master of the King's Music at the court of Charles II. In the fall of 1673 Cambert founded in London a so-called Royal Academy of Music in which he held the post of director. This institution was an essentially private opera theater, although Cambert appears to have enjoyed for a time a measure of royal patronage, which may have included a loan of stage sets. The high-sounding name Cambert chose for the theater was undoubtedly intended to reflect some of the authority of the Parisian operatic monopolies and apparently served its purpose at least posthumously by misleading historians into attributing to Cambert an official position as royal director of music at Charles's court.

In the early spring of 1674, Cambert's Royal Academy presented his opera *Ariane,* which had been modified with the assistance of Grabu, at the new Royal Theatre in Bridge's Street (Drury Lane). This theater had been built to replace a predecessor that was destroyed by fire in 1672. It appears that *Ariane* was performed in French by a troupe of French musicians who had been assembled by the Academy. Cambert's destiny to remain obscure was mirrored by the libretto, published in London in 1674, which identifies Grabu as the sole composer. The libretto bears a prefatory letter to Charles II dedicating the work of the Academy to his service and is signed, perhaps too optimistically, "your Academy of Music." It may be that other of Cambert's works were performed in London in his early years there. It is possible that *Pomone* and *Les Peines et Plaisirs de l'Amour* were also produced in London, and a surviving libretto attributes to Cambert's pen a portion of a *Ballet et Musique pour le Divertissement du Roy de la Grande Bretagne* performed at the court in 1674.

Unfortunately, Cambert's royal favor seems to have been short-lived. In August 1674, his mainstay at the court, Grabu, was abruptly dismissed as Master of the King's Music and replaced by Nicholas Staggins, an Englishman. After 1674 Cambert is lost from sight until April 1677, when *Le Mercure Galant* reported his death with a resounding eulogy: "Let us say that Music is unfortunate this year in every way, and that if some musicians have lost their lawsuits, others have lost their lives. M. Cambert, master of music of the late Queen Mother, has died in London, where his genius was greatly esteemed. He had received many benefits from the King of England and from the greatest noblemen at his Court, and all that they had seen of his work did not belie in the least what he had done in France. It is to him that we owe the establishment of the operas that we see today." This obituary did not impute to Lully a role in Cambert's death. However, both in his historical assessment of Cambert's achievement and in a possibly ironic linking of Cambert's death to another man's suffering at the hands of Lully, the writer appears to have intended to identify Cambert in death both as the superior of Lully and as his enemy. The assertion that France owed to Cambert the establishment of its operas obviously amounted to a rejection of Lully's claims to that distinction. Not content with this critical judgment, the article delivered a personal blow against Lully by comparing Cambert's loss of life to another musician's loss of a lawsuit. This reference was clearly to Lully's judicial persecution of Henri Guichard, a business associate of Pierre Perrin who had held an interest in Perrin's theater and royal opera franchise.

Lully, in order to counter Guichard's opposition to his opera monopoly, had initiated a criminal proceeding against Guichard for an alleged attempt to murder him by the administration of poisoned snuff. The poisoning plot, if it existed at all, was carried forward with all the clumsiness one associates with murder conspiracies in opera librettos. If there was any truth in the accusation, it is likely that the plot was, after feeble beginnings, largely an invention of Lully himself for the purpose of entrapping his adversary. The allusion in *Le Mercure*'s Cambert obituary to Lully's legal victory was based on the fact that Guichard had been convicted of the attempted poisoning in September 1676, but the comment was premature: Guichard appealed and was exonerated by the appellate court within a month after the appearance of the article. However, the association made between Cambert's death and Lully's own charge of foul play against Guichard was to bear fruit in the creation of a murder legend.

Lully died in 1687, and his death was marked by both praise and bitter invective. One of the most extravagant literary tributes was an account of Lully's reception into the Elysian Fields by the great departed spirits of music. Possibly in response to this piece or similar exercises in hyperbole, poet and humorist Antoine Bauderon de Sénecé published in 1688 a satirical account of what *really* happened to Lully in the Elysian Fields. Sénecé's book is in the form of a letter from the sixteenth-century court poet Clément Marot to a fictional editor, circumstantially specifying as place and date of mailing "Elysian Fields, April 20." In describing Lully's entry into the Temple of Persephone, Sénecé, like the Cambert obituary writer, makes a reference to Lully's charges against Guichard, and he leaves no doubt as to his feeling with regard to their lack of substance: "Barely had he [Lully] taken a few steps when he was seen to change color and to show on his countenance more fear than he had ever had for the alleged poison of Guichard."

Persephone's Temple was the Elysian tribunal at which judgment was passed on the qualification of a new entrant to be granted immortality. Lully's advocate was the Italian musician Balthasar de Beaujoyeulx, who, like Lully, had found favor at the French court. Beaujoyeulx appears to have been a rather maladroit spokesman, since he spiced his eulogy with Sénecé's own animus. When the ancient Greek poet Anacreon opposed Lully's claims on the ground that Lully refused to recognize the primacy of the poet's contribution to opera, Beaujoyeulx rejoined that Lully was well aware of the important role of poetry: why else would he have headed his scores with laudatory verse epistles to Louis XIV?

At this point Perrin's ghost stepped forward and, still bitter over the loss of opera rights to Lully, urged that, far from being entitled to immortality, Lully should be punished "as the thief that he was of the labors and reputations of others." Perrin's final charge that Lully had used his opera monopoly to "cut the throat of so many" is immediately taken up in a melodramatic intervention by the tortured ghost of Cambert:

"Yes, yes, cut the throat!" a furious shade cried in a terrifying outburst, and, breaking through the crowd, was immediately recognized as that of poor Cambert, still entirely disfigured by the wounds that he had received when he was in England. "You see, Madame," he continued in the same tone, "to what end I was brought by the tyranny of Lully. The applause that I received from the public for the merit of my compositions aroused his indignation. He wanted to seize the fields that I had prepared, and reduced me to the cruel necessity of going to seek my bread and glory in a foreign court, where envy found a way of finishing, by depriving me of life, the crime that it had begun by exiling me from my homeland. But regardless of whose hand struck the blows that took my life, I shall never impute them to anyone but Lully, whom I regard as my real murderer, and against whom I demand that you give justice. And it is not for myself alone, Madame, that I implore your equity; it is in the name of all those who distinguished themselves in their times by some rare ability in music, whom he never ceased to persecute by all sorts of means."

Like the *Mercure* obituary, this passage can be read as falling far short of a murder accusation against Lully. The "crime" of which Lully is most clearly accused is that of having driven Cambert into exile by unfair competition, and in Sénecé's view this crime also entails moral responsibility for Cambert's death in exile, regardless of the identity of the actual assailant. But the author's reference to "envy" as a common element in the crimes of exile and murder created an ambiguity. Did Sénecé mean to imply that minions of Lully pursued Cambert to London to complete his destruction, or that Cambert fell victim of envy from musical circles in London as he had done in Paris?

The various strands of Sénecé's innuendos were taken up by later historians, and his fictional account of a lacerated ghost became the surrogate of a corpus delicti. The historians do not acknowledge their debt to Sénecé, and it is understandably embarrassing to footnote an assertion of murder by reference to a satirist. But the mark of *The Letter of Clément Marot* is everywhere to be seen in the commentaries on Cambert's death from the eighteenth century on. In 1705 Le Cerf de La Viéville, a great admirer of Lully, developed the anti-English possibilities of Sénecé's charges, perhaps in the belief that he would thereby deflect blame from Lully. While Sénecé had left ambiguous the source of the "envy" that had destroyed Cambert, Le Cerf pointed his finger directly at Cambert's English competitors:

Cambert seeing himself of no use in Paris after the establishment of Lully, moved to London, where his *Pomone,* which he presented there, attracted to him considerable evidences of friendship and favor from the King of England and the greatest nobles of the Court. But the envy that is inseparable from merit cut short his days. The English do not find it good for a foreigner to intrude into their entertainment and instruction. The poor fellow died there a little earlier than he would have died elsewhere.

The brothers Parfaict in their *Histoire de l'Académie royale de musique* paraphrased the above passage from Le Cerf de La Viéville and also referred to a rival tradition that Cambert had been murdered by a valet. This accusation (a parallel to the familiar mystery novel formula that "the butler did it") leaves open the question as to whether the servant was acting for himself or for an undisclosed principal, and some whispered that the murderer was engaged by Lully. In addition to all the mysteries this theory summons up as to the details of the hiring and escape of the murderer, the valet legend makes us wonder how Cambert, obscure as he was in 1677, could have afforded a manservant.

A less sensational residue of the Sénecé lampoon is a suggestion that Cambert died of heartbreak in his London exile. This version leaves those who adopt it free to blame Lully or not, depending on their views of Lully's musical merits and of the fairness of the steps he took to win and enforce his operatic monopoly.

Although none of the modern authorities attributes Cambert's death to Lully, a surprising number assume that Cambert was murdered. No evidence is cited in support of this assumption, and it is hard to escape the conclusion that it is based solely on Sénecé's book. The writers accepting Sénecé may well have asked: would Sénecé have dared describe the bleeding Cambert while his survivors still lived if Cambert had died peacefully or in his sleep? After all, it is one thing to speculate about a poisoning when a man has died suddenly (as in Mozart's case) and quite another to make vivid reference to knife wounds when Cambert's family presumably had seen his body and could tell the public whether he had been stabbed.

In view of the fact that Cambert's allegedly violent end came in London, it is odd that the tradition of his murder appears to be an exclusively French product. My researches in London libraries and record offices have not uncovered any evidence either that Cambert was murdered or that there were any rumors to such effect current in London at the time of his death. Although exhaustive searches might prove more successful, I have not found any English record of his death or burial. At the time of his death, burial records were maintained by individual parishes, of which there were more than one hundred in London and its environs. None of the published or unbound parish burial registers for London or Middlesex County that I have reviewed contains any record of Cambert's death or burial, nor do the will indexes list any will in his name. In fact, the only surviving official English record I have discovered with relation to the Cambert family in or after 1677 is a note in the State Domestic Papers of the grant of a passport for France to Cambert's daughter, Marianne, on December 1, 1678.

Cambert's death came too early in journalistic history for us to expect to find a story on his death (however lurid it might have been) in the London newspapers. The most important journal, the semi-official *London Gazette,* devoted most of its space to news of the wars of Louis XIV. Unfortunately, however, it contains no news of Cambert's death. Accounts of murders were not considered appropriate daily fare for the *Gazette's* readers. However, if Cambert had indeed been murdered by a valet who had committed the additional capital offense of stealing plates or linens from his master's household, notice of the theft would have been permitted to appear among the *Gazette's* frequent advertisements for runaway servants and stolen household goods.

The absence of newspaper coverage of crime in the late seventeenth century was compensated for by a welter of pamphlets devoted to murders and executions. These pamphlets are indexed by Donald Goddard Wing in his bibliography of seventeenth-century publications. The name of Cambert does not appear in the index. There is no reference to criminal proceedings arising out of Cambert's death in the selective edition of the records of the Middlesex Sessions, and a search made at my request of the surviving indictments in the Court of King's Bench during the Hilary Term of 1677 (January–March 1677) was also unproductive.

And the principal English diarists also make no reference to Cambert's death. Robert Hooke, friend of Sir Christopher Wren and Samuel Pepys, was in London in early 1677 and made daily entries in his diary during the period. He was an aficionado of crime, if we can judge by an entry in 1677 referring to "H. Killigrews man stabbd next the Kings bedchamber" and by his speculation in a 1679 diary page on the motive for the murder of Sir Edmundbury Godfrey. However, Hooke's diary does not mention Cambert's death.

Therefore, in the scales against Bauderon de Sénecé's vivid description of Cambert's wounds we place the English silence. This silence is capable of conspiratorial interpretation, particularly if we accept the strand of French tradition that implies that Cambert was disposed of by English rivals. However, it is a strain on credulity to suppose that conspirators, however highly placed, could have imposed a total censorship not only on official records but also on gossip, one of the most highly developed arts in London. If we are to reconcile the possibility of Cambert's murder with the apparent disregard of his death in London, we must hypothesize that by 1677 Cambert had fallen into obscurity, that his murderer was unknown and went unpunished, and that there was no inquiry into the circumstances of his death. In view of the difficulties presented in researching the records of this period, these possibilities cannot be excluded. However, unless evidence of murder should someday be discovered in England, it will remain difficult to accept not only the libels against Lully in the matter of Cambert's death but also the more widely accepted hypothesis that he died a violent death by someone's hand.

A century after Cambert's death, Sir John Hawkins set down what can still serve as the official English view of the Cambert affair. According to Hawkins's account, Cambert "died, with grief, as it is said, in 1677." The source of his grief was the rejection of his work by the English public. Hawkins found no fault with the public's judgment. Ironically, Hawkins paired the antagonists Lully and Cambert as coworkers in a style that could not fall pleasingly on English ears:

> Perhaps one reason of the dislike of the English to Cambert's *Pomone,* was that the opera was a kind of entertainment to which they had not been accustomed. Another might be that the levity of the French musical drama is but ill suited to the taste of such as have a relish for harmony. The operas of Lully consist of recitatives, short airs, chiefly gavots, minuets, and courants, set to words; and chorusses in counterpoint, with entrées, and splendid dances, and a great variety of scenery; and, in short, were such entertainment as none but a Frenchman could sit to hear, and it was never pretended that those of Cambert were at all better.

Hawkins's chauvinistic rejection of French taste was matched by his outrage at the tradition, stemming from Le Cerf de La Viéville, that Cambert had been done away with by envious English musicians. Referring to a republication of Le Cerf's innuendo in Bourdelot's music history originally published in 1715, Hawkins comments wryly on the hypothesis that English musicians envied Cambert: "A modest reflexion in the mouth of a man whose country has produced fewer good musicians than any in Europe."

It is appropriate that this tale of the musical animosities of Italy, France, and England should end on a note of nationalism.

Bibliographical Notes

The Gluck–Piccinni rivalry is discussed in Alfred Einstein, *Gluck* (New York: Collier, 1962), 162–69. For an analysis of the tradition of Mozart's murder, see "Salieri and the 'Murder' of Mozart," chapter 2 in this volume. An excellent description of the cultural centralism that fostered Lully's control over French opera is presented in Robert M. Isherwood, *Music in the Service of the King: France in the Seventeenth Century* (Ithaca: Cornell Univ. Press, 1973), 170–247.

The two principal theoretical works contrasting the French and Italian styles as developed in the late seventeenth century were Abbé François Raguenet's *Parallèle des Italiens et des Français* (Paris, 1702) and Jean-Louis Le Cerf de La Viéville's *Comparaison de la musique italienne et de la musique française,* 3 parts (Brussels: F. Foppens, 1705–06). The best biographical works on Lully are those by Henry Prunières: *Lully* (Paris: Laurens, 1909) and the fictionalized *La Vie Illustre et Libertine de Jean-Baptiste Lully* (Paris: Plon, 1929). Later biographies appear to be highly derivative from Prunières, for example R. H. F. Scott, *Jean-Baptiste Lully: The Founder of French Opera* (London: Peter Owen, 1973); Eugène Borrel, *Jean-Baptiste Lully* (Paris: La Colombe, 1949). For appraisals of Cambert's contributions to French opera, see Arthur Pougin, *Les Vrais Créateurs de l'Opéra Français: Perrin et Cambert* (Paris: Charavay, 1881); Charles Nuitter et Ernest Thoinan, *Les Origines de l'Opéra Français* (Paris: Plon, 1886). References to Cambert's career in London are drawn from André Tessier, "Robert Cambert à Londres," *La Revue Musicale,* Dec. 1927, 101, 110–11, 118; W. H. Grattan Flood, "Quelques précisions nouvelles sur Cambert et Grabu à Londres," *La Revue Musicale,* Aug. 1928, 351.

Musicologist Philippe Beaussant, in *Lully ou Le musicien du Soleil* (Paris: Gallimard, 1992), provides a balanced assessment of Cambert's talent and tribulations: "What shall we say about Cambert? Without making him, as some have believed themselves able to do, the great genius shamefully evicted by Lully, the 'true founder' of French opera, despoiled of his work, let us say that he deserved better than the misfortune that never ceased to pursue him and his bad luck in having Perrin as a librettist" (453).

The posthumous tribute to Lully referred to is *Le triomphe de Lully aux Champs-Elysées* (1687), reprinted in a special Lully issue of *La Revue Musicale,* Jan. 1925, 90. I have translated passages from the first edition of Antoine Bauderon De Sénecé, *Lettre de Clément Marot à Monsieur de . . . touchant à ce qui s'est passé, à l'arrivée de Jean Baptiste de Lulli, aux Champs Elysées* (Cologne, 1688), 32–33, 51–53. For Le Cerf's theory of Cambert's death, see his *Comparaison de la musique italienne et de la musique française,* part 2:177. The brothers Parfaict are quoted in Pougin, *Les Vrais Créateurs,* 250n1. See also Romain Rolland, *Les Origines du Théâtre Lyrique Moderne—Histoire de l'Opéra en Europe avant Lully et Scarlatti* (Paris, 1931), 259n3. An example of the "heartbreak" theory of Cambert's death is found in Castil-Blaze (François Henri Joseph Blaze), *Molière Musicien* (Paris: Castil-Blaze, 1852), 2:126.

In the course of my research, I reviewed all of the parish records published by the Harleian Society as well as the unbound parish records for London and Middlesex County in the possession of the Society for Genealogists in London. I also consulted will records at the Guildhall Library, the County Hall, and the Middlesex Record Office. The reference to Marianne Cambert's passport is in Calendar of State Papers, Domestic Series, Mar. 1, 1678 to December 31, 1678 (London, 1913), 614. The record reflects the grant of a passport to "Marie du Moulier and Marianne Cambert." It is possible that the first name is a misprint of the maiden name of Cambert's widow, Marie de Moustier.

I am indebted to records agent Stephen Goslin for the search of the King's Bench Records.

The comments of Sir John Hawkins are drawn from his *General History of the Science and Practice of Music* (London: T. Payne, 1776), 4:239n. For Bourdelot's republication of Le Cerf's innuendo, see *Histoire de la Musique et de ses Effets, depuis son origine, jusqu'à présent,* begun by Abbé Pierre Bourdelot, continued by Pierre Bonnet-Bourdelot, and completed and published by Jacques Bonnet (Amsterdam, 1725), 3:163–64.

Charles Burney also cites a French music history source for the statement that "Cambert, who died in London in 1677, broke his heart on account of the bad success of his operas in England." Charles Burney, *A General History of Music from the Earliest Ages to the Present Period* (London, 1789), 4:188.

2

Salieri and the "Murder" of Mozart

On October 14, 1791, in his last surviving letter, Wolfgang Amadeus Mozart wrote to his wife, Constanze, at Baden that he had taken the Italian composer Antonio Salieri and singer Mme Cavalieri to a performance of *The Magic Flute* and that Salieri had been most complimentary: "from the overture to the last chorus there was not a single number that did not call forth from him a bravo! or bello!" Less than two months later, Mozart was dead. In a report from Prague written within a week of the composer's death, the *Musikalisches Wochenblatt* mentioned rumors of poisoning based on the swollen condition of his body. Suspicion gradually came to focus on Salieri, who, despite his recently professed delight over *The Magic Flute,* had for a decade been an implacable rival of Mozart's in Vienna. In the years prior to Salieri's death in 1825, the rumors of his recourse to poison as a final weapon of rivalry were fed by reports that, while in failing health, he had confessed his guilt and, in remorse, had attempted suicide.

The rumors that Mozart was murdered and that Salieri was his assassin have produced controversies and traditions in the fields of medicine, musicology, history, and literature that have not lost their vigor today. In 1970 David Weiss's novel *The Assassination of Mozart* appeared in bookstores, and Peter Shaffer's play *Amadeus* (1979) and the film version brought the poisoning contentions to the notice of an international audience. Medical and historical debate on Mozart's untimely demise continues both in this country and abroad, and German writers and researchers in particular show a remarkable preoccupation with the composer's death. The writings on this fascinating subject differ widely in quality and point of view, and many of the authors seem unaware of the sources on which others have drawn. It therefore remains tempting to return to this classic historical mystery with a view to providing a "confrontation" among the various contending parties, including those who blame Mozart's death on natural causes, poisoning, professional jealousy, Viennese politics, the Masons, and the Jews. In this centuries-long debate no possible suspect is spared. Virtually no organ of Mozart's body is regarded as above the suspicion of having failed in its appointed function, and, with the exception of the composer's wife, no group or individual is cleared of complicity in his death.

The story of Mozart's last days must begin with the mysterious commissioning of the Requiem, which apparently caused his sensitive soul to brood on death. Around July of 1791, when Mozart's work on *The Magic Flute* was virtually complete and rehearsals had already begun, Mozart received a visit from a tall, grave-looking stranger dressed completely in gray. The stranger presented an anonymous letter commissioning Mozart to compose a requiem as quickly as possible at any price. It is now accepted that the commission had a very prosaic explanation. The messenger's patron was Count Franz von Walsegg, who wanted a requiem composed in memory of his late wife and who intended to pass himself off as the composer. Mozart accepted the commission but put aside his work on it when he received an offer to write an opera, *La Clemenza di Tito*, for the coronation of Emperor Leopold in Prague. Just as Mozart and his wife were getting into the coach to leave for Prague, the gray-clad messenger appeared "like a ghost" and pulled at Constanze's coat, asking her, "What about the Requiem?" Mozart explained his reason for the journey and promised to turn to the Requiem as soon as he came back to Vienna.

Franz Niemetschek, Mozart's first biographer, reports that Mozart became ill in Prague and required continuous medical attention while he was there. He states that Mozart "was pale and his expression was sad, although his good humour was often shown in merry jest with his friends."

On Mozart's return to Vienna, he started work on the Requiem with great energy and interest, but his family and friends noted that his illness was becoming worse and that he was depressed. To cheer him up Constanze went driving with him one day in the Prater. According to her account, which she gave to Niemetschek, "Mozart began to speak of death, and declared that he was writing the Requiem for himself. Tears came to the eyes of this sensitive man. 'I feel definitely,' he continued, 'that I will not last much longer; I am sure I have been poisoned. I cannot rid myself of this idea.'" This conversation, which is one of the cornerstones of the poisoning legend, Constanze later repeated to her second husband, Georg Nikolaus von Nissen, who recorded it in his biography of Mozart in much the same terms as the Niemetschek version. And Constanze was still recounting the episode as late as 1829, according to the journal of Vincent and Mary Novello, who paid her a visit in Salzburg that year. In fact, the Novellos' journal reveals that Constanze told them Mozart had clearly identified the poison that he thought had been administered to him as aqua toffana. This poison, whose principal active ingredient is supposed to have been arsenic, was introduced by a Neapolitan woman named Toffana in seventeenth-century Italy and had startling effect on the statistics of sudden death. It is perhaps regrettable that history has not seen fit to choose the most sublime of her various nicknames for the potion, the "manna of St. Nicholas di Bari."

One of the most dependable accounts of Mozart's terminal illness is provided by Constanze's sister, Sophie Haibel, in a report sent in 1825 to Nissen at his request for use in his biography. Most of the symptoms with which the medical historians have dealt we owe to her account: the painful swelling of his body, which made it difficult for him to move in bed; his complaint that he had "the taste of death" on his tongue; his high fever. Despite his suffering, he continued to work on the Requiem. On the last day of the composer's life, when Sophie came to see him, Franz Xaver Süssmayr was at his bedside and Mozart was explaining to him how he ought to finish the Requiem. (It is reported by a newspaper article contemporaneous with Sophie's memoir that earlier on this day Mozart was singing the alto part of the Requiem with three friends who supplied falsetto, tenor, and bass.) Mozart retained his worldly concerns to the point of advising Constanze to keep his death secret until his friend Johann Georg Albrechtsberger could be informed, so that his friend could make prompt arrangements to succeed to Mozart's recently granted rights as colleague and heir apparent of the Kapellmeister of St. Stephen's Cathedral. When Mozart appeared to be sinking, one of his doctors, Nikolaus Closset, was sent for and was finally located at the theater. However, according to Sophie's account, that drama lover "had to wait till the piece was over." When he finally arrived, he ordered cold compresses put on Mozart's feverish brow, but these "provided such a shock that he did not regain consciousness again before he died." According to Sophie, the last thing Mozart did was imitate the kettledrums in the Requiem. She wrote that thirty-four years later she could still hear that last music of his.

Nissen, in his biography, states that Mozart's fatal illness lasted for fifteen days, terminating with his death around midnight (probably the early morning) of December 5, 1791. The illness began with swellings of his hands and feet and an almost complete immobility, and sudden attacks of vomiting followed. Nissen describes the illness as "high miliary fever." He writes that Mozart retained consciousness until two hours before his death.

Neither Dr. Closset nor Mozart's other attending physician prepared a death certificate with the cause of death stated. No autopsy was performed. From the very beginning, doctors and other commentators have differed widely as to the cause of death. Nissen's identification of the fatal illness as miliary fever accords with the cause of death as set forth in the registers of deaths of St. Stephen's Cathedral and Parish in Vienna. Although that nomenclature does not fit any precise modern medical definition, it is surmised that the term as used in the medicine of the eighteenth century denoted a fever accompanied by a rash. However, a number of other illnesses have been put forward as the cause of death, including grippe, tuberculosis, dropsy, meningitis, rheumatic fever, heart failure, and Graves' disease. The hypotheses of some of these diseases, such as tuberculosis, appear to have been based not so much on any of the observable medical phenomena as on a biographical conclusion that Mozart in his last years was killing himself with overwork and irregular living. The suggestion of Graves' disease, a hyperthyroidism, is derived from facial characteristics of Joseph Lange's unfinished 1782 portrait of the composer, which include, in the words of an imaginative medical observer, "the wide angle of the eye, the staring, rather frightened look, the swelling of the upper eyelid and the moist glaze of the eyes." Art historian Kenneth Clark has quite a different interpretation of Mozart's intent gaze in the Lange portrait. The painting conveys to Clark not the sign of death nine years off but "the single-mindedness of genius."

Probably the prevailing theory of modern medical authorities who believe Mozart to have died a natural death is that he suffered from a chronic kidney disease, which passed in its final stages into a failure of kidney function, edema, and uremic poisoning. This theory was advanced as early as 1905 by a French physician, Dr. Barraud. It is argued that this diagnosis is most in keeping with the recorded phenomena of Mozart's last suffer-

Unfinished portrait of Wolfgang Amadeus Mozart, by Joseph Lange, his brother-in-law, 1782. Credit: Corbis.

ings, including the swelling of his body and the poisonous taste of which he complained. Modern medicine has established that certain chronic diseases of the kidneys are commonly caused by streptococcal infections suffered long before the effect on the kidney function becomes noticeable.

Medical commentators on Mozart's death have implicated a number of childhood illnesses as likely contributors to his chronic kidney disease. They are aided in their researches by detailed descriptions of the illnesses of the Mozart children in the letters of their father, Leopold. Certainly their recurring health problems were a proper subject of parental concern, but the pains Leopold takes to describe his children's symptoms and the course of their illnesses and recoveries stamp him as an amateur of medicine. In fact, he often administered remedies to the children, his favorites being a cathartic and an antiperspirant he refers to as "black powder" and "margrave powder," respectively. It is fortunate that the children survived both the diseases and their father's cures.

In 1762, when Wolfgang was six years old, he was ill with what a doctor consulted by Leopold Mozart declared to be a type of scarlet fever, an infection capable of causing kidney injury. In the following year, 1763, young Mozart contracted an illness marked by painful joints and fever, which have led some observers to postulate rheumatic fever, which could also lead to adverse effects on the kidney. When Mozart was nine he took sick with what Leopold called a "very bad cold," and later the same year both his sister and he were more seriously ill. Nannerl was thought to be in such serious condition that the administration of extreme unction was begun. No sooner had she recovered than Wolfgang was struck by the illness, which in his father's words reduced him in a period of four weeks to such a wretched state that "he is not only absolutely unrecognizable, but has nothing left but his tender skin and little bones." Some modern commentators identify this severe illness as an attack of abdominal typhus. Two years later, in 1767, Wolfgang contracted smallpox, which left him quite ill and caused severe swelling of his eyes and nose. He also suffered throughout his childhood from a number of bad toothaches, which have led some supporters of the kidney disease theory to invoke the possibility of a focal infection contributing to kidney damage. The last reference to an illness prior to his final days is in a letter from Leopold to Nannerl in 1784, when her brother was twenty-eight. This letter reported that Wolfgang had become violently ill with colic in Vienna and had a doctor in almost daily attendance. Leopold added that not only his son "but a number of other people caught rheumatic fever, which became septic when not taken in hand at once." There is no other evidence of a serious illness of Mozart's until the period of a few months preceding his death. Dr. Louis Carp attempts to demonstrate the presence of severe symptoms of kidney disease as early as 1787 by quoting from a letter from Mozart to his father in April of that year: "I never lie down at night without reflecting that—young as I am—I may not live to see another day." This letter, written to console Mozart's dying father, gives us an important insight into the composer's speculations about mortality. However, it does not provide any clue to his physical condition or to his feelings about his health.

Locked in combat with the medical authorities attributing Mozart's death to disease is a substantial body of modern physicians who would support Mozart's own suspicion by declaring that he was indeed poisoned. These doctors, including Dieter Kerner and Gunther Duda of Germany, believe that the poison administered was mercury, which attacks the kidneys and produces much the same diagnostic picture as that presented by the final stages of a natural kidney failure. Both Kerner and Duda minimize much of the evidence that has been cited in support of the theory that Mozart suffered from a chronic kidney disease stemming from streptococcal infection. Dr. Duda believes that the severity and nature of Mozart's childhood illnesses have been misstated. He is convinced that the so-called scarlet fever identified as such by the physician whom Mozart's father consulted was, in fact, erythema nodosum, a disorder of uncertain origin resulting in raised eruptions of the skin and of far less severity than scarlet fever. Moreover, Duda is not at all certain that Mozart's other illnesses, which have been regarded as outbreaks of rheumatic fever, were not common cases of the grippe. Unimpressed by the speculation that Mozart's toothaches may have involved harmful focal infections, he points out that Mozart's sister, who was exposed to and suffered most of the same childhood illnesses as Mozart, lived to the age of seventy-eight. Duda also emphasizes the lack of evidence that Mozart himself had any substantial illness between 1784 and the last year of his life.

Dr. Kerner believes that the characteristics of Mozart's last illness more closely resemble those of mercury poisoning than of the last stages of a chronic kidney illness. No contemporaries relate that Mozart complained of thirst, which Kerner associates with chronic nephritis. He also notes that Mozart was conscious until shortly before his death, worked actively to the last, and, during the final months of his life, composed some of his greatest masterpieces. In contrast with this spectacular creative activity, it is Kerner's experience that "uremics are always for weeks and usually months before their death unable to work and for days before their death are unconscious." Kerner accepts the contemporary report that Mozart first became ill in Prague and assumes that small doses of mercury were given to him in the summer of 1791, followed by a lethal dose close to the time of his death. Noting that in the Vienna of Mozart's time mercury was in limited use as a remedy for syphilis, Kerner states that such use was introduced by Dr.

Antonio Salieri, who appears here as more distinguished than murderous. Credit: Corbis.

Gerhard van Swieten, whose son Mozart knew. From such observations a commentator has erroneously read the Kerner study as arguing that Mozart poisoned himself in an effort to cure himself of syphilis.

It is hard for a modern reader of these arguments to rid himself of the prejudice against regarding a poisoning as anything but an exotic possibility. Unfortunately, and for good experiential reasons, it was not so regarded in the eighteenth century. Gunther Duda, in an effort to prepare his readers to accept his thesis, begins his book with the reminder that before firearms became generally available, poison was an extremely common weapon, and the subtle art of its use well-known. It is remarkable how many of Mozart's contemporaries who figure in some manner in the controversies over his death regarded poisoning or suspicion of poisoning as risks to be taken quite seriously.

Even if the medical evidence and eighteenth-century experience do not exclude the poisoning of Mozart as a possibility, there has always been difficulty in identifying a murderer and finding an appropriate murder motive. Salieri has always been the prime candidate for the unhappy role of Mozart's murderer. He fits this assignment imperfectly at best. Although (in large part due to the effect of the murder legend) time has not been kind to Salieri's musical reputation, he was undoubtedly one of the leading composers of his period and an important teacher of composition, counting among his pupils Beethoven, Schubert, Liszt, Hummel, Süssmayr, and Meyerbeer. He was also a famous teacher of singing. All his students loved and respected him. Friends remembered him as generous, warm, and kind-hearted, and he even had the ability to laugh at himself (at least at his difficulties with the German language). He must have had a way with people, since he apparently established a close personal relationship with the difficult Beethoven.

However, the musicians whose careers Salieri helped to forward shared an advantage that Mozart lacked—they all had the good fortune not to be competitors of Salieri in the composition of Italian opera. There seems little question but that he was a formidable professional opponent of Mozart, although they appear to have been able to sustain correct and even superficially friendly social relationships. Salieri enjoyed a competitive supremacy over Mozart and many other aspiring composers in Vienna, and only partly because of the undoubtedly high regard in which his contemporaries held Salieri's own operatic works. Of far greater importance in his ascendancy was the fact that because of his favor with Joseph II until the emperor's death in 1790, and because of his successive roles as court composer, director of the Italian Opera, and court conductor, Salieri was able to wield powerful influence over the availability of theaters and patronage. Mozart, his father, and many of their contemporaries believed that Salieri had caused the emperor to be unfavorably disposed toward *The Abduction from the Seraglio* and had also been responsible for the later plot (fortunately unsuccessful) to induce the court to hamper the opening of *The Marriage of Figaro*. In his letters to his father, Mozart also accused Salieri of having prevented him from obtaining as a piano pupil the princess of Württemberg. In December 1789 Mozart wrote to his fellow Freemason and benefactor, Michael Puchberg, that next time they met he would tell him about Salieri's plots "which, however, have completely failed."

Although Mozart was undoubtedly very sensitive about barriers to his career, his feeling that Salieri used court influence to frustrate his musical competitors is borne out in the memoirs of tenor Michael Kelly and librettist Lorenzo da Ponte, who worked with both Mozart and Salieri and were on friendly terms with each. Kelly refers to Salieri as "a clever, shrewd man, possessed of what Bacon called crooked wisdom" and adds that Salieri's effort to have one of his operas selected for performance instead of *The Marriage of Figaro* was "backed by three of the principal performers, who formed a cabal not easily put down." Da Ponte blames attempts to disrupt rehearsals of *Figaro* on the opera impresario Count Orsini-Rosenberg and a rival librettist, Casti, rather than directly on Salieri, although both men appear to have been in Salieri's camp. He also remarks that before he came to the rescue, "Mozart had, thanks to the intrigues of his rivals, never been able to exercise his divine genius in Vienna." Da Ponte was a slippery man with an elastic memory; it is probably fair to attribute to him the assessment of Salieri that he claimed to have heard from the lips of Emperor Leopold: "I know all his intrigues. . . . Salieri is an insufferable egoist. He wants successes in my theatre only for his own operas and his own women. . . . He is an enemy of all composers, all singers, all Italians; and above all, my enemy, because he knows that I know him."

Nevertheless, there is much to suggest that Salieri's hostility toward Mozart did not extend to the sphere of personal relations. He was one of the small group of mourners who followed Mozart's coffin as it was carried from the funeral service at St. Stephen's Cathedral toward the cemetery, making a greater display of public grief over Mozart's death than Constanze, who stayed at home, supposedly still overcome by her husband's death. Moreover, Salieri later became the teacher of Mozart's son Franz Xaver Wolfgang and in 1807 gave him a written testimonial that procured him his first musical appointment.

It is difficult to decide whether Constanze or the Mozart family gave any credence to the rumors against Salieri. Would Constanze have entrusted the musical education of her son to a man she believed to be the murderer of his father? Nissen's biography contains an allusion to Salieri's rivalry but rejects the poisoning charges. Nissen reports that Constanze attributed Mozart's suspicion of poisoning to illness and overwork. Moreover, he included in his biography an anonymous account of Mozart's early death that was published in 1803. The quoted article dismisses the possibility of poisoning and attributes Mozart's fears to "pure imagination." Nissen's biography was undoubtedly written and compiled with Constanze's blessing. However, as witnessed by her conversations with the Novellos, which took place at approximately the same time as the appearance of the biography, Constanze never put Mozart's suspicions out of her mind. Her preoccupation with this subject reappears a decade later in a letter written to a Munich official, quoted by Kerner in his study, to the effect that "her son Wolfgang Xaver knew that he would not, like his father, have to fear envious men who had designs on his life." Her other son, Karl, on his death in 1858, left behind a handwritten commentary in which there is further discussion of the poisoning of Mozart—this time by a "vegetable poison."

The views of Mozart's contemporaries as to Salieri's guilt doubtlessly divided along lines of personal or musical loyalties. In the years 1823 through 1825, partisans of Salieri rallied to the defense of his reputation in the face of widely circulated reports that he had confessed to the murder and attempted suicide by cutting his throat. When Kapellmeister Johann Gottfried Schwanenberg, a friend of Salieri's, was read a newspaper account of the rumor that Mozart had fallen victim of Salieri's envy, he shouted, "Crazy people! He [Mozart] did nothing to deserve such an honor." But believers in the poisoning rumors were tireless and ingenious in spreading their gospel. At a performance of Beethoven's Ninth Symphony in Vienna on May 23, 1824, leaflets containing a poem that pictured Salieri as Mozart's rival "standing by his side with the poisoned cup" were distributed to concertgoers. Giuseppe Carpani, a friend of Salieri and an early biographer of Haydn, responded with an effective public relations campaign on behalf of his maligned compatriot. He published a letter he had received in June 1824 from Dr. Guldener, who had not attended Mozart but had spoken to Mozart's physician, Dr. Closset. The latter had advised him, Guldener wrote, that Mozart's fatal illness had been a rheumatic and inflammatory fever that attacked many people in Vienna in 1791. Dr. Guldener added that in view of the large number of people who had seen Mozart during his illness and the experience and industry of Dr. Closset, "it could not have escaped their notice then if even the slightest trace of poisoning had manifested itself." (Presumably Dr. Closset was quite industrious after theater hours.) Carpani appended the text of Guldener's letter to his own article defending Salieri's innocence. The Salieri press campaign also included a statement by the two men who served as Salieri's keepers in his last years of declining health. They attested that they had been with him day and night and had never heard him confess the murder.

The views of Beethoven on the poisoning rumors have always been intriguing because of his love of Mozart's music and his friendship with Salieri. We know from the entries in his conversation books that Beethoven's callers gossiped about the case with him. In late 1823 publisher Johann Schickh referred to Salieri's unsuccessful suicide attempt. In the following year Beethoven's nephew Karl and his friend and future biographer Anton Schindler discussed the reports of Salieri's confession of the poisoning, and Karl, in May 1825, the month of Salieri's death, mentioned the persistence of the rumors. It is generally agreed that Beethoven did not believe Salieri was guilty. He was fond of referring to himself as Salieri's pupil, and after Mozart's death he dedicated the violin sonatas Opus 12 (1797) to Salieri and wrote a set of ten piano variations on a duet from Salieri's charming opera *Falstaff* (1798). Nevertheless, wagging tongues delighted in passing along a spurious anecdote that Rossini, when he had induced Salieri to take him to visit Beethoven at his Vienna home, was angrily turned away at the door with the words, "How dare you come to my house with Mozart's poisoner?"

The irony of the Beethoven–Rossini anecdote lies in the fact that the lives of both men were touched by fears and rumors of poisoning. Beethoven believed that his hated sister-in-law Johanna had poisoned his brother and intended to poison his nephew. Rossini's mourning for the early death of his friend Vincenzo Bellini in Paris was followed by rumors of poisoning, as was Salieri's attendance at Mozart's funeral. But the Bellini poisoning legend was cut down in its infancy as a result of decisive action on the part of Rossini. Francis Toye writes that "Rossini, unwilling, perhaps, to figure as a second Salieri, insisted on an autopsy, which put an end to the rumor once and for all." It almost appears that Salieri was the only musical protagonist in the case who is not reported to have been subject to fears of poisoning. However, we have the intriguing biographical note that Salieri, though from a land of wine, drank only water. His modest drink, unlike headier beverages, would have given his taste buds early warning should an enemy have surreptitiously added a splash of aqua toffana.

Most of Mozart's principal biographers have either held aloof from the poisoning theory or rejected it outright. Franz Niemetschek appears to straddle the issue. Although he purported to blame lack of exercise and overwork for Mozart's death, he left room for a more sinister possibility: "These were probably the chief causes of his untimely death (if, in fact, it was not hastened unnaturally)." He also attributed Emperor Joseph's critical remarks about *The Abduction from the Seraglio* to "the cunning Italians" and added that "Mozart had enemies too, numerous, irreconcilable enemies, who pursued him even after his death." These enemies, including Salieri, were still alive, and Niemetschek, whatever his suspicions, could not very well have gone much further in pointing a finger.

Edward Holmes was the first to exonerate Salieri expressly. He relegated the poisoning legend to a footnote and concluded that "Salieri, the known inveterate foe of Mozart, was fixed upon as the imaginary criminal." Otto Jahn, in his great study of Mozart, continued to keep the charges of poisoning imprisoned in a footnote and referred to the suspicions of Salieri's guilt as "shameful." Hermann Abert preserves Jahn's fleeting reference to the murder legend and observes that Mozart's suspicion of poisoning evidenced his "morbidly overstimulated emotional state." Arthur Schurig blames Mozart's death on a severe grippe. Alfred Einstein not only fails to dignify the poisoning tradition by any mention but even finds the only explanation for Salieri's animosity in Mozart's "wicked tongue." Eric Blom and Nicolas Slonimsky have rejected the possibility of murder but have fortunately taken the trouble to chronicle some of the excesses of the various murder theories. However, both Russia and Germany have in our time produced writers who claim to have found "historical" evidence that not only supports the murder thesis but reveals a political motive for the crime and for the prevention of its detection.

Soviet musicologist Igor Boelza (or Belza), in his brochure *Motsart i Sal'eri,* published in Moscow in 1953, exhibits a chain of hearsay evidence to the effect that Salieri's priest made a written report of his confession to the murder. He claims that the late Soviet academician Boris Asafiev told him that he had been shown the report by Guido Adler, also deceased. Boelza states that Adler had also spoken of the document to "colleagues and numerous scholars," none of whom is named in the brochure. According to Boelza, Adler engaged in a detailed study of the dates and circumstances of the meetings of Mozart and Salieri and established that they bore out the facts of the confession and satisfied the classic element of "opportunity." But Adler apparently was no more ready to publish his Inspector French–style timetable than he was willing to publish the Salieri confession itself. It is small wonder that Alexander Werth, in commenting on Boelza's book, remarks, "It looks as if the Adler mystery has taken the place of the Salieri mystery."

Boelza also seeks support for the murder case in the mysterious circumstances of Mozart's funeral and burial, which German writers like to refer to as *die Grabfrage* (the burial question). Posterity has always been puzzled by the fact that only a few friends (including Salieri) accompanied the funeral procession, and that even they turned back before arriving at the cemetery. The burial was that of a poor man, and Mozart's body was placed in an unmarked grave. These bitter facts, so inappropriate to memorializing the passing of a great genius and a man who had loving friends and family, have been variously explained, and even the explanation least flattering to Mozart's circle usually falls short of implication of criminal conduct. Constanze's absence and the mourners' desertion before the cemetery gates have traditionally been blamed on a wintry storm, but this explanation is belied both by a contemporary diary and by an intelligent modern inquiry made by Nicolas Slonimsky at the Viennese weather archives. Nissen does not mention the weather in his biography and attributes Constanze's absence to her overpowering grief. The poverty of the burial has sometimes been taken to reflect the stinginess of Mozart's friends and patrons, notably of Baron van Swieten, though others have claimed that the burial was in keeping with the surviving spirit of decrees of Emperor Joseph II enacted in 1784 and repealed in the following year. These decrees, inspired by the reforming emperor's dislike for the pomp of burial, had provided that the dead not be buried in coffins but merely sewn in sacks and covered with quicklime and had also abolished most of the funeral ceremonies.

In Boelza's version, all the events of Mozart's interment take on a more sinister significance. He conjures up a plot headed by Baron van Swieten and joined by all of the composer's acquaintances and relatives (with the exception of Constanze). On van Swieten's orders, all the mourners departed on the way to the grave and the body was intentionally interred in unmarked ground. In supplying a motive for this strange plot to suppress traces of the murder, Boelza brings the case into the political arena and adds a Marxist twist. It seems that van Swieten was afraid that "nationalist upheavals" would result if the working masses of imperialist Vienna learned of the report that Mozart had been poisoned by a court musician and, what was worse, by a foreigner.

German writers have produced a rival tradition that Mozart was murdered by his Freemason brethren. The Masonic murder theory apparently originated in 1861 with Georg Friedrich Daumer, a researcher of antiquities and a religious polemicist. Daumer's work was elaborated in the Nazi period, notably by General Erich Ludendorff and his wife, Mathilde, who were so fired by enthusiasm for their revelations that they devoted the family press to the propagation of their indictment of the Freemasons.

The case against the Freemasons takes a number of lines. Daumer claimed that Mozart had not fully carried out Masonry's "party line" in *The Magic Flute*. Mozart, in his view, had offended the Masons by his excessive attachment to the figure of the Queen of the Night and by his use of Christian religious music in the chorale of the Men of Armor. Daumer also believed that the murder thwarted Mozart's plan to establish his own secret lodge, to be called "The Grotto." Mathilde Ludendorff built on Daumer's imaginings. She preferred, however, another explanation of the Masons' outrage at *The Magic Flute*. She believed that Mozart had hidden beneath the pro-Masonic surface of the opera a secret counterplot that depicted Mozart (Tamino) seeking the release of Marie Antoinette (Pamina) from her Masonic captors. Mathilde Ludendorff, like Igor Boelza, added an element of nationalism. She claimed that the murder was also motivated by the opposition of the Freemasons to Mozart's hope of establishing a German opera theater in Vienna. Both Daumer and Mathilde Ludendorff related Mozart's death to other murders of famous men in which they likewise saw the Masonic hand at work. Daumer's conviction of the correctness of his view of Mozart's death was reinforced by his belief that the Freemasons had also murdered Lessing, Leopold II, and Gustav III of Sweden (who was assassinated at the famous masked ball only a few months after Mozart's death). Mathilde Ludendorff expanded this list of victims to include Schiller and, in a virtuoso display of freedom from chronology, Martin Luther as well.

It is not surprising that the Ludendorff writings have a heavy overlay of anti-Semitism. General Ludendorff claimed that the secret of Masonry was the Jew and that its aim was to rob the Germans of their national pride and to ensure the "glorious future of the Jewish people." He attempted to establish a Jewish role in Mozart's murder by commenting mysteriously that Mozart had died "on the Day of Jehovah." The combination of anti-Semitic and anti-Masonic prejudices had been common since the nineteenth century and was intensified at the turn of the century in the heat of passions generated by the Dreyfus affair. It is ironic to observe this marriage of hates in retroactive operation in the Mozart case, since

Masonic lodges of the eighteenth century generally excluded Jews from membership. There is reason to speculate, at least, that Mozart himself did not develop the racist insanity so many of his countrymen showed in later periods of history. Paul Nettl observes that if he had done so, the world would have lost the fruits of his collaboration with the talented Jewish librettist Lorenzo da Ponte. To be regarded as further evidence of Mozart's receptivity to the ideas of Jewish writers is the catalog of his library of books left at his death, which lists a work on the immortality of the soul by Moses Mendelssohn.

The anti-Masonic murder theory, like the Boelza theory, assumes a conspiracy of Mozart's friends and family. Mathilde Ludendorff incriminates Salieri, van Swieten, and even the mysterious messenger who commissioned the Requiem. She accuses this oddly assorted group of slowly poisoning Mozart and of employing Nissen to cover up the crime in his biography. Constanze is, as a good and loyal housewife, spared any suggestion of involvement. However, as in Boelza's theory, her absence from the burial and its strange character are removed from the plane of personal and financial circumstance and explained by the conscious design of the conspirators. Frau Ludendorff even supplies the ghoulish hypothesis that the burial conformed to requirements of Masonry that the body of a transgressor against its laws must be denied decent burial.

Strangely enough, the Masonic murder legend has also been denied burial. Dr. Gunther Duda, whose medical views of the case have already been cited, is a "true believer" in the research of Daumer and the Ludendorffs. His book *Gewiss, man hat mir Gift gegeben* ("I am sure I have been poisoned"), a comprehensive study of Mozart's death written in 1958, is prefaced with a quotation from Mathilde Ludendorf. He views the charges against the Masons as having been established with the same compelling force as a mathematical or logical formula. He supports the condemnation of the Masons by the following syllogism, all of the links in which he accepts as fact: (1) Mozart was a Mason; (2) the Masonic lodges claimed the right to sentence disobedient members to death; (3) Mozart was a disobedient member; and (4) the execution of the Masonic death sentence is evidenced by Mozart's death, the manner in which he died, and the circumstances of his burial. However, Duda's zeal for his cause carries him well beyond the bounds of medical history or even plain logic. Faced with the question of why the Masons would have punished only Mozart but not the librettists of *The Magic Flute* as well, he notes with suspicion the sudden deaths of the two men who may have collaborated on the libretto. The principal librettist, Emanuel Schikaneder, died in 1812 (twenty-one years after the opera's premiere), and Karl Ludwig Gieseke, who may also have had some role in shaping the libretto, died in 1833. Duda must surely be suggesting that the Freemasons had at their disposal the slowest poison in the annals of crime.

Kerner, in the 1967 edition of his study of Mozart's death, does not expressly join in the accusations against Freemasonry. However, his sober medical discussion passes at the end of his work into a vapor of astrology and symbolism that may enshroud suggestions of conspiracy. He points out that a "Hermes stele" pictured on the left side of an engraving on the frontispiece of the first libretto of *The Magic Flute* contains eight allegories of Mercury, the god who gave his name to the poison that Kerner believes killed Mozart. The engraving was made by the Freemason Ignaz Alberti. The allusion to Mercury in Alberti's frontispiece indicates to Kerner that more people were "in the know" about the murder than is generally assumed. He demonstrates the continuity of this secret knowledge over the centuries by observing that the special Mozart postage stamp issued by Austria in 1956 shows eight Mercury allegories in its frame. Kerner passes from iconography to alchemy and then to sinister hints. He states that in the symbolism of the alchemists, the number eight as well as the color gray represented the planet Mercury, "which reawakens lively associations of thought with the 'Gray Messenger,' who often put Mozart in fear in his last days."

Neither Dr. Duda nor Dr. Kerner attempts to reconcile with the Masonic murder theory their shared medical assumption that Mozart's poisoning began in the summer of 1791, before *The Magic Flute* was first performed. Moreover, if Mozart was out of favor with his Masonic brethren, a mind disinclined to conspiratorial thinking would find it hard to explain either the commission he received shortly before his death to compose a Masonic cantata or the emotional oration that was delivered to a Masonic lodge in memory of Mozart and was printed in 1792 by the very same Freemason Alberti whose "Hermes stele" struck Kerner as suspicious.

The elements of conspiratorial thinking and exoticism have recently been supplied in abundant measure. Since the publication of their separate research, Kerner and Duda have, in collaboration with Johannes Dalchow, written two books that make more explicit their incrimination of the Masons as the murderers of Mozart. As elaborated in *Mozarts Tod* (1971),

Masonry's involvement in Mozart's death was complex and premeditated. According to the authors (who in this respect, as in many others, parrot the writings of Mathilde Ludendorff), the "gray messenger" ordering the Requiem was not the agent of Count von Walsegg but an emissary of the Masons announcing their death sentence. What was the reason for Mozart's murder? The authors provide two possibilities and like them both so well they do not choose between them: (1) a "ritual murder" in which Mozart was offered as a sacrifice to the Masonic deities; and (2) a punishment of Mozart by the Masons, with the participation of Salieri, for the crime of having revealed Masonic secrets in *The Magic Flute*. The authors engage in an extended numerological exegesis of *The Magic Flute* that they believe proves the Masonic murder (and presumably also Mozart's acceptance of his execution). The authors assert that the number eighteen is paramount in the music and libretto of the opera, by intentional association with the eighteenth Rosicrucian degree of Masonry, and that Mozart's death was also scheduled to give prominence to this number. It is observed with triumph by Kerner and his colleagues that Mozart's Masonic cantata was performed on November 18, 1791, exactly eighteen days before his death! Amid all this mystification the medical research of the authors has come to play a minor role, and the bigoted spirit of Mathilde Ludendorff lives again.

The novelists have, since the very year of Salieri's death, had a field day with the theme of the poisoning. The succession of bad novels that stress the poisoning has continued unabated to our own day; certainly in the running for honors as the worst novel on the poisoning is David Weiss's *The Assassination of Mozart,* which summons up a vision (straight out of John Le Carré and Len Deighton) of a reactionary Austrian regime giving tacit approval to Salieri's murder of Mozart and ruthlessly suppressing every attempt to investigate the crime.

However, the poisoning tradition has produced one authentic masterpiece, Pushkin's short dramatic dialogue *Mozart and Salieri,* conceived in 1826 (only one year after Salieri's death), when the rumors of his confession were still in the air, and completed in 1830. In the Pushkin play (later set by Rimsky-Korsakov as an opera), Salieri poisons Mozart both because Mozart's superior gifts have made Salieri's lifelong devotion to music meaningless and because Mozart has introduced Salieri's soul to the bitterness of envy. Unlike many of Mozart's later admirers, Pushkin does not depict Salieri as a mediocre hack but rather as a dedicated musician who was intent on the perfection of his craft and who was able to appreciate innovative genius (as in the case of his master, Gluck) and to assimilate it into his own development. However, Salieri refers to himself as a "priest" of music to whom his art is holy and serious. He is enraged by Mozart's free, creative spirit and by what he sees as Mozart's lighthearted, almost negligent, relation to the products of his genius. Salieri's assessment of his rival is confirmed for him by the joy Mozart takes in a dreadful performance of an air from *Figaro* by a blind fiddler. As was true in their real lives, both Salieri and Mozart in Pushkin's pages inhabit a world where poisoning is assumed to be a possible event even in the lives of famous and civilized men. Mozart refers to the rumor that "Beaumarchais once poisoned someone," and Salieri alludes to a tradition that Michelangelo committed murder to obtain a dead model for a crucifixion. In Pushkin's play the murder of Mozart brings no relief for Salieri's torment but only furnishes final proof of his inferiority. At the close of the play Salieri is haunted by Mozart's observation immediately before being poisoned that "genius and crime are two incompatible things."

Even if we suspect that the play has attributed to Salieri more subtlety as a criminal than he displayed in years of crude plotting against Mozart's musical career, Pushkin possibly comes closer to explaining how Salieri could have made a confession of guilt than does the inconclusive medical evidence or reference to Viennese court intrigue or Masonic plots. Salieri might have recognized the depth of the animosity he had harbored. He might have come to the understanding that, if the essential life of a divinely gifted composer is in his art, he and others who had stood again and again between Mozart and his public had, with malice aforethought, set out to "murder" Mozart. Pushkin's view of the criminality of selfish opposition to artistic greatness is incisively stated in a brief comment he wrote in 1832 on the origin of the poisoning legend. Pushkin records that at the premiere of *Don Giovanni,* the enthralled audience was shocked to hear hissing and to see Salieri leaving the hall "in a frenzy and consumed by envy." The note concludes: "The envious man who was capable of hissing at *Don Giovanni* was capable of poisoning its creator."

There is more reason to attribute to Salieri the symbolic crime of attempted "murder" of a brother artist's work than to speculate that Salieri was a poisoner. This judgment would be supported by the testimony of Ignaz Moscheles. Moscheles, who was a former pupil of Salieri and who loved him dearly, visited the old man in the hospital shortly before his death.

According to Moscheles's account, Salieri hinted at the poisoning rumors and tearfully protested his innocence. Although Moscheles wrote that he was greatly moved by the interview and that he had never given the rumors the slightest belief, he added the following comment: "Morally speaking he [Salieri] had no doubt by his intrigues poisoned many an hour of Mozart's existence." In his fictional account of the Salieri protestation, Bernard Grun attributes Moscheles's comment about moral guilt to Salieri himself, thus harmonizing the interview with the rumors of Salieri's "confession." According to the Novellos' journal, Mozart's son Franz Xaver Wolfgang expressed a similar view, namely that Salieri had not murdered his father but that "he may truly be said to have poisoned his life and this thought . . . pressed upon the wretched man when dying."

If Moscheles's narrative is accepted, many events become easier to explain. Salieri's delight over *The Magic Flute* may have been genuine. It is possible that even in Mozart's lifetime Salieri finally acknowledged Mozart's genius and tempered his own feeling of rivalry. Tardy recognition of Mozart's greatness (and, perhaps, regret for their estrangement) may also account for Salieri's attendance at the funeral and his kindness to Mozart's son.

If Salieri was guilty of hostility toward Mozart's art but not of poisoning the artist, his punishment can only be called "cruel and unusual." After all, Salieri's plots against Mozart's fame ultimately failed, and yet he was long punished—by reason of the evil legend that clings to his name—with almost total obscurity for his own music. For many years only minor instrumental works of Salieri were available on commercial recordings. The situation is now changing for some of the operas that made Salieri's reputation, including *Les Danaïdes* and *Falstaff,* which have been released on CDs. Perhaps the time has arrived to turn from the documentation of Mozart's death to a closer investigation of the music of Salieri. Perhaps such a study will provide evidence that even without his adroitness in Viennese opera politics and his prestigious positions, Salieri would have afforded substantial musical competition to Mozart.

Bibliographical Notes

An English translation of letters of Mozart and his family is Emily Anderson, ed. and trans., *The Letters of Mozart and His Family,* 2 vols., 2nd ed. (New York: St. Martin's Press, 1966). Leopold Mozart's administration of "black powder" and "margrave powder" to young Wolfgang is referred to in a letter of October 30, 1762 (p. 9).

A selective list of reminiscences and biographies of Mozart include: Hermann Abert, *W. A. Mozart,* 2 vols., 7th ed. (Leipzig: Breitkopf and Härtel, 1955–56), 2:693; Georg Friedrich Daumer, *Aus der Mansarde* (Mainz: Verlag von Franz Kirchheim, 1861), 4:1–184; Otto Erich Deutsch, *Mozart: A Documentary Biography,* 2nd ed. (Palo Alto, Calif.: Stanford Univ. Press, 1966), 432, 523; Alfred Einstein, *Mozart: His Character, His Work* (New York: Oxford Univ. Press, 1965), 86; Edward Holmes, *The Life of Mozart* (1845; reprint, London: J. M. Dent, 1939), 279n1; Otto Jahn, *The Life of Mozart,* trans. Pauline D. Townsend, 3 vols. (London: Novello, Ewer, 1882), 3:354n7; Lorenzo da Ponte, *Memoirs of Lorenzo da Ponte* (New York: Orion, 1959), 67, 100; Charlotte Moscheles, ed., *Recent Music and Musicians as Described in the Diaries and Correspondence of Ignatz Moscheles* (New York: Holt, 1873), 59; Franz Niemetschek, *Life of Mozart* (London: Leonard Hyman, 1956), 43; Georg Nissen, *Biographie W. A. Mozarts* (Leipzig: G. Senf, 1828), 563–64, 572; Vincent Novello and Mary Novello, *A Mozart Pilgrimage* (London: Novello, 1955), 125, 127–28; Michael Kelly, *Reminiscences of Michael Kelly,* 2 vols. (1826; reprint, New York: Da Capo, 1968), 1:254; Arthur Schurig, *Wolfgang Amade Mozart,* 2 vols. (Leipzig: Insel-Verlag, 1923), 2:374.

Books and articles on the death of Mozart include the following sources in English, German, and Russian: Carl Bär, *Mozart-Krankheit-Tod-Begräbnis* (Salzburg: Salzburger Druckerei, 1966); Eric Blom, "Mozart's Death," *Music and Letters* 38 (1957): 320–26; Igor Boelza (Belza), *Motsart i Sal'eri* (Moscow: Muzgiz, 1953), and Boelza's supplementary 1962 essay, *Motsart i Sal'eri (Ob istoricheskoi dostovernosti tragedii Pushkina),* http:feb-web.ru/feben/pushkin/serial/im4/im4-237-htm?cmd=2 (accessed July 23, 2009); Johannes Dalchow, Gunther Duda, and Dieter Kerner, *W. A. Mozart—Die Dokumentation seines Todes* (Pähl: Bebenburg, 1966), and *Mozarts Tod 1791–1971* (Pähl: Hohe Warte Bebenburg, 1971); Gunther Duda, *"Gewiss, man hat mir Gift gegeben"* (Pähl: Hohe Warte, 1958); Dieter Kerner, *Krankheiten Grosser Musiker* (Stuttgart: Schattauer, 1967); C. G. Sederholm, "Mozart's Death," *Music and Letters* 32 (1951): 345; Nicolas Slonimsky, "The Weather at Mozart's Funeral," *Musical Quarterly* 46 (1960): 12–21; William Stafford, *The Mozart Myths: A Critical Reassessment* (Palo Alto, Calif.: Stanford Univ. Press, 1991); Alexander Werth, "Was Mozart Poisoned?" *New Statesman,* Apr. 14, 1961, 580, 582.

Ties between anti-Semitism and anti-Masonic prejudice are considered in Paul Nettl's *Mozart and Masonry* (New York: Philosophical Library, 1957), 85.

Art historian Kenneth Clark commented on Joseph Lange's portrait of Mozart in Clark's *Civilisation* (London: British Broadcasting Corp., 1971), 240.

Salieri's character is rehabilitated in Volmar Braunbehren's *Maligned Master: The Real Story of Antonio Salieri* (New York: Fromm International, 1992).

Three scientific researchers have recently concluded that Mozart died of a streptococcal infection contracted in an epidemic of that affliction in Vienna: Richard H. C. Zegers, Andreas Weigl, and Andrew Steptoe, "The Death of Wolfgang Amadeus Mozart: An Epidemiologic Perspective," *Annals of Internal Medicine* 151, no. 4 (Aug. 18, 2009), 274–78. The authors surmise that the streptococcus led to an acute nephritic syndrome.

Among novels based on Mozart's death are: Bernard Grun, *The Golden Quill* (New York: Putnam, 1956), wherein Grun attributes Moscheles's comment about Salieri's "moral guilt" to Salieri himself (366); Michael Levey, *The Life and Death of Mozart* (New York: Stein and Day, 1971); David Weiss, *The Assassination of Mozart* (London: Hodder and Stoughton, 1970).

The two principal dramas based on the "murder" of Mozart are Alexander Pushkin, *Mozart and Salieri*, in *The Poems, Prose and Plays of Alexander Pushkin* (New York: Random House, 1936); and Peter Shaffer, *Amadeus* (London: André Deutsch, 1980).

In the revision of *Amadeus* for American audiences, the elderly Salieri, contemplating suicide, asserts that he is innocent of murdering Mozart but has been falsely confessing the crime so as to be remembered in infamy. See Albert Borowitz, *Terrorism for Self-Glorification: The Herostratos Syndrome* (Kent, Ohio: Kent State Univ. Press, 2005), 140–41.

3

Finale Marked Presto: The Killing of Leclair

The murder of Jean-Marie Leclair, eighteenth-century composer and violin virtuoso, is a mystery worthy of Agatha Christie. The Paris detective forces headed by Lieutenant of Police Antoine Gabriel de Sartine picked their way through a maze thickly populated with suspicious characters and lying witnesses and, to make their path more difficult, encountered many red herrings. The motive for the crime was perhaps the most bewildering enigma of all; the investigators were compelled to consider the possibility that Leclair's sudden death was due to robbery, marital discord, professional hostility, or perhaps the dark act of a sardonic psychopath.

In 1764 the sixty-seven-year-old Leclair would have been justified in resting on the laurels of his distinguished career. Born in 1697 in Lyon, the eldest of eight children of a master lace maker, he reportedly made his debut as a dancer at Rouen. He later followed his father's profession for a while in his native city, where he married the daughter of a liquor merchant in 1716. In 1722 he went to Turin to serve as principal dancer and ballet master. It was in the Turin theater that he mounted his first stage works, mythological ballets composed in the popular taste of the time. He then returned to Paris, where in 1723 he published his earliest work of instrumental music (which was to be his principal genre); this maiden effort was a book of sonatas for violin and basso continuo. Five years later Leclair made a brilliant debut as a violinist in the Concert Spirituel. About that time he published a second book of sonatas in which his characteristic and frequent use of double stops showed the influence of the violinist Giovanni Battista Somis, with whom he had studied at Turin. Leclair's first wife died, and in 1730 he married Louise Roussel, a music engraver who had published some of his works.

Leclair's career continued to blossom. Beginning in 1733 he performed in the Royal Orchestra, where he encountered a formidable rival, violinist Pierre Guignon. Neither of them wanted to play second fiddle to the other's first violin, so they agreed to change places on a regular monthly rotation. Guignon allowed Leclair to begin the new arrangement by occupying first place. However, it is said that when Leclair's month had run out he resigned from the orchestra rather than pass to the second rank.

After leaving the Paris orchestra, Leclair spent several years in Holland under the sponsorship of Princess Anne of Orange and of François du Liz and was subsequently called to the court of Don Philip of Spain at Chambéry. In 1746 Leclair's only opera, *Glaucus et Scylla,* was performed with moderate success at the Paris Opéra. In about 1749 he came under the protection of his last patron, the Duke de Gramont, who had established a fashionable theater in his villa at Puteaux. Here Leclair served as first violinist and contributed ballet pieces and divertissements to its repertory.

By the end of the next decade, a streak of misanthropy, quite in the style of Molière, seems to have afflicted Leclair. In 1758 he left his wife and lived alone in a house on the rue de Carême-Prenant in a northeast suburb of Paris near what is now the St. Martin Canal. It was a small, ramshackle two-story structure situated within a walled garden entered through a gate from the street. The Duke de Gramont was concerned about the dangerous circumstances of his favorite musician living in seclusion and many times offered Leclair lodging at his own residence. According to Barnabé Farmian Durosoy, the principal authority on Leclair's last years, the composer was going to accept the offer, but he was not fated to do so.

At about 6:00 A.M. on October 23, 1764, Louis Bourgeois, a sixty-four-year-old gardener, passed by Leclair's garden gate and noticed that it was open. This seemed strange—but not strange enough to overcome his early-morning appetite, and he went on to his regular place for breakfast. On his way back he met Jacques Paysant, who tended Leclair's garden, and told him about the open gate. Shortly afterward, Paysant appeared at Bourgeois' house in obvious distress. In the garden he had found his employer's hat and wig lying on the ground. Fearing some calamity, he did not dare enter the house alone and wanted Bourgeois to accompany him. They summoned other neighbors and, buoyed by the strength of numbers, returned to the garden. Near the front door of the house lay the hat

Jean-Marie Leclair. Engraving by Jean-Charles François after Alexis Loir, 1741.

and wig, as Paysant had said. The door was open, and even before they entered the vestibule they could see Leclair's body.

He was lying on his back on the floor of the vestibule in front of the staircase, with his bare head resting against the door leading to the cellar.

He was dressed in ordinary street attire—gray jacket, a vest, two shirts (one heavy and decorated and the other of mousseline), trousers, black woolen stockings, and shoes with copper buckles. His shirts and camisole were stained with blood. He had been stabbed three times by a pointed instrument: above the left nipple, in the lower stomach on the right side, and in the middle of his chest. Frightened by what they found, the witnesses locked the garden gate. Paysant ran to notify Mme Leclair and Leclair's son-in-law, the painter Louis Quenet. Within an hour Mlle Nigotte Petitbois, the Leclairs' goddaughter, arrived after having alerted Commissaire Thiot at the Paris police headquarters in the Châtelet. She was accompanied by a lawyer named Godard, whom one of her neighbors had summoned. Quenet arrived shortly afterward.

The police investigation, under the immediate direction of Commissaire Thiot and Inspector Hubert Receveur, was soon in full swing. Jacques-Pierre Charles, master in surgery, was called in to examine the body. He observed bruises in the lumbar area and on the lips and jawbone, which tended to show that, after a struggle with his assailant, Leclair had been thrown onto his back. His body had been surrounded by a number of oddly assorted objects that seemed to have been deliberately arranged by the murderer to create a bizarre mise-en-scène, much in the manner of whodunnit authors of the 1930s. In addition to the hat and the wig, the police found near the vestibule door a roll of blank music manuscript paper and a book (apparently from the victim's own library) on which the hat had been placed. The book was a collection of witticisms entitled *L'Elite des bon mots.* Caught up in a trellis outside the vestibule door, the police also found a hunting knife with its bare, unstained blade pointed downward; it fit precisely the scabbard attached to the sash Leclair wore. At a corner of the trellis, which showed no signs of being disturbed, the police came on another knife lying on the ground. It was a blunt table knife and appeared to be stained only with rust.

A search of Leclair's pockets turned up a snuff box (with only two pinches left), a black leather case containing a pair of spectacles, a bread roll, and two handkerchiefs, one of them wrapped around a meat sandwich. It was observed that his gilded copper watch was missing. The detectives surmised that the murderer might have taken the watch to lay a false trail, for they ransacked the house without uncovering any evidence of theft or breaking and entering. It was noted, however, that many of the shutters of the windows facing the garden were open and that two panes of the first-story window were half open; one of the leaves of the vestibule door had been found ajar by the original investigators. In the locked drawer of a commode in Leclair's bedroom, the police found four louis d'or of twenty-four livres and two and a half louis in six-franc crowns—a cache of money sufficient to rule out burglary as a motive for the crime. Nevertheless, the garden and adjacent properties were also examined for possible evidence of a nocturnal intrusion. The police observed that about a foot of the coping of the garden wall facing the house was damaged; the plaster was detached, and many pieces of it lay on the ground of Leclair's garden and his neighbor's. It was also noticed that behind the wall on the left of Leclair's garden (on the property belonging to the father of the gardener Bourgeois) there was a large mass of earth mold that would have made it very easy to pass over the wall onto Leclair's premises. The police determined, however, that the mold had been placed there a very long time ago.

One of the central mysteries of the murder scene, the role played by the house keys in the fatal encounter, is not clarified in the surviving police archives. However, the testimony of Jeanne Louise Aubert, a sixty-year-old widow living on the rue de Carême-Prenant, suggests that keys to both the vestibule and garden door may have been found on the premises. She testified that when Leclair's neighbors left the house after discovering the body, they locked the vestibule door and gave the key to her for safekeeping pending the arrival of the family. She also noticed on leaving the house that the latchkey to the street gate was resting on the trellis.

The police also investigated reports of movements of strangers in the neighborhood on the night of the crime. Pierre Dangreville, a sentry on duty nearby that evening, noticed a driverless carriage drawn by two horses coming from the direction of Paris toward the suburbs; it stopped at the corner of Leclair's street. He approached the carriage and found it laden with pottery. About a quarter of an hour later, two soldiers who appeared to be on guard duty stopped in the middle of the road near the rue de Carême-Prenant. Dangreville observed them closely, concerned that they might steal the pottery. But they did not show the slightest interest in the vehicle. One of them passed beyond the carriage into the rue de Carême-Prenant and was lost to view; about fifteen minutes later he returned, running to rejoin his comrade. It was raining very hard, and Dangreville had assumed that this was the reason for his haste. While the soldier was absent, Dangreville heard no cries or noise from the direction of Leclair's street. A few moments later the soldiers' patrol appeared, and they rejoined its ranks on the way back to the city. Later that night the mystery of the driverless pottery carriage was solved: Dangreville was introduced to a cart driver, who inquired about the carriage. He said that after he entered a cabaret about 9:00 P.M. to have a drink, the horses wandered off. Police efforts to determine the identity of the suspicious soldier were fruitless.

Another mysterious stranger was seen on the night of the crime by Rose Pelletier, the wife of mounted patrolman Antoine Claude. At about 10:00 P.M., while entering the rue de Carême-Prenant on her way home from a visit to the Bourgeois family, she saw a large man standing with his back against a garden wall. He was dressed in a black or gray coat and had brown unpowdered hair. He frightened her, and she hurried home.

For the most part the police inquiries as to Leclair's actions immediately before the crime were not illuminating. As was his custom, Leclair had played several games of billiards on Monday evening, October 22, at the establishment of Pierre Lamotte. Lamotte recalled that at 9:30 P.M. Leclair invited him to join him for supper at an inn and, after he declined, bid him good night. At about 9:45 Leclair entered Charles Roussel's food shop and purchased a roll, perhaps having decided to dine alone. From his sentry box Pierre Dangreville saw Leclair light a candle within a little paper lantern and proceed on his way home. His last stop before reaching his house was at the neighboring shop of Jean Thibault, where he purchased a ball of twine.

Inspector Receveur was able to account for the probable sources of the money found in Leclair's commode. Mme Leclair told him that she had given Leclair some funds about ten days earlier and that M. Geoffroy had given him five louis about two days before his death. An intriguing piece of information was supplied by the café keeper, Roussel. On Sunday, October 14, Leclair had awakened him around midnight and asked him for the duplicate house key he had left with him about eighteen months earlier for safekeeping. He told Roussel that either someone had stolen his keys at a theatrical performance or that he had lost them during the day.

From the many dubious figures referred to in the police interrogations, two principal suspects emerged. The first was Leclair's gardener, Paysant, who aroused the interest of the investigators with his lies, misleading testimony, and defensive, hostile gossip. When no watch was found on Leclair's body, Paysant claimed that Leclair had not possessed one for eighteen months. But Lamotte, the proprietor of the billiard parlor, told the police that he had seen Leclair consult his watch before leaving the parlor on the night of the crime. Paysant also swore that Leclair had no money, a statement contradicted by the testimony of others and by the police's discovery of cash in Leclair's commode. The gardener also may have given inaccurate information about the time of his discovery of the body and his whereabouts on the night of the murder. He asserted that he had first seen the open garden gate at 6:00 A.M., but other witnesses stated that Paysant and Bourgeois had awakened them as early as 4:30 to ask their help in inspecting Leclair's house. Paysant also informed the police that he had returned home at 7:30 P.M. on October 22, but his mistress told a woman named Laborgne that he had not actually come back until 10:30, perhaps a half hour after Leclair had completed his evening's purchases and arrived at his house.

The gardener's talkativeness also weighed against him. He remarked to one of the neighbors whom he had enlisted to visit Leclair's house on the morning of October 23 that perhaps Leclair had an attack of colic, to which he was prone, and had died for want of assistance. He repeated this when the body was discovered, even though the blood-drenched shirt should have convinced him that a more violent incident had occurred. Paysant was not present at the burial of his employer in the St. Laurent Church on October 25, and his brother drew many questioning looks by his efforts to eavesdrop on the conversations of those in attendance. At the very moment when the body was to be lowered into the grave, a woman from Leclair's neighborhood exclaimed, "M. Paysant told me that he would do the same to my husband."

Questioning by the investigators indicated that the gardener's odd behavior might be partly due to his having a police record that he feared might bring him under suspicion. Paysant also remarked that this was the second time he had had the misfortune of having an employer die during his service. However, Paysant's past encounters with the police had nothing to do with murder or other serious crimes. He had been jailed for some minor scrape during his service in a regiment of the French Guard and had been brought before the Châtelet as the putative father of an illegitimate child borne by a woman of bad reputation with whom he had lived for many years.

Paysant's worries about his past inspired him not only to equivocate about his own actions and knowledge but also to suggest a rival suspect to the police. Why not, he suggested, investigate the Duke de Gramont himself? The duke had often visited Leclair in his presence, he said, and the gardener drank wine with both of them. This testimony, when the duke heard of it, drove him to fury. The gossip about his drinking in ill-assorted company had the ring of truth about it, for he was reputed to be a drunkard who "looked as if nature had intended him for a barber." But he did not care to be branded an alcoholic or a murderer and dashed off an angry (and misspelled) letter to Lieutenant Sartine: "It has come to my attention through the nephew of M. Leclair that his gardener said to Commissaire Guiot [*sic*] in his interrogations that he had seen me many times with M. Leclair and that the three of us had often drunk together. I have been at M. Leclair's house only twice and I have never drunk or eaten there. Besides such company is not made for me. Furthermore, for about seven or eight years I have drunk nothing but water. A man who, in order to clutch at straws as best he can, says whatever comes into his head is a man to be mistrusted."

The police briefly arrested Paysant, but his release was ordered by the Châtelet. He undoubtedly was an untrustworthy witness, but there was little ground to consider him guilty of murder.

A more likely suspect was Leclair's nephew, mentioned in the duke's letter. François Guillaume Vial, aged forty, was the son of Leclair's sister Françoise. Himself a musician, he came to Paris around 1750 and, abetted and pampered by Mme Leclair, never tired of beseeching his uncle to find him a post in the musical service of the Duke de Gramont. On many occasions Vial gave vent in the bitterest terms to his resentment of his uncle's failure to advance his career. Among letters discovered at Leclair's house, Inspector Receveur discovered four in which Vial asked Leclair's pardon for grave offenses against him. But even his uncle's murder could not induce him to moderate his expressions of grievance. He told the surgeon Charles that "his uncle had done him many injustices and had refused to introduce him to the Duke de Gramont." To Mme Roussel he asserted that Leclair "had only received what he deserved, having always lived like a wolf" and that "he had always hoped to die suddenly." To Tetart, the mounted patrolman who was on duty at the Leclair house, Vial delivered a tirade of abuse against his dead uncle. Leclair, he said, was a recluse who "didn't want to see anyone from the family and desired to die suddenly, even by murder"; he "had never wanted his nephew to have a career or to give him his protection," but now that Leclair was dead, "he [Vial] was going, thank God, to have a career!" When Tetart proposed to Vial that he view the body, he refused, stating that "he knew very well what it was like."

Vial was anxious to establish an alibi for himself at the time of the crime. He said that he had arrived in Paris from Conflans (where he claimed to have gone to see the archbishop) and that on his return to Paris he had found waiting for him at home a *procureur* who advised him of his uncle's death. He added that it was fortunate for him that he was not in Paris at the time of the murder, for otherwise people might perhaps have said that he was the guilty party. Inspector Receveur visited the archbishop and discovered that Vial's alibi was a complete and shameless fabrication. He had not been to Conflans on the date of the crime, and he was unknown to the archbishop, the members of the archbishop's household, and the religious community of Conflans. The methodical Receveur confirmed these facts through interviews, not only with the archbishop's lackeys and *valets de chambre* but also with the mother superior of the neighboring convent. Receveur returned from Conflans resolved to redouble his measures to investigate Vial's actions.

The inspector's suspicions of Leclair's nephew were strengthened by his strange behavior at his uncle's funeral. According to Receveur, "a trembling and astonishing agitation on the day of burial called him to the attention" of police and others who were in attendance. To make matters worse, Vial had apparently attempted to influence the testimony of other witnesses in a direction that he may have thought favored his own alibi. Desnos, a soldier on guard at the Leclair house, saw Vial take the gardener Bourgeois aside and heard him say that he should not tell the police he had seen the garden gate open between 4:00 and 5:30; others, Vial whispered, had already testified that they had not seen the gate open until 6:00 or 6:30, and there was no point in creating contradictions in statements on the subject. Receveur also noted in his summary of the evidence that Vial's physique appeared to match that of the large man dressed in black who had been seen moving along Leclair's wall on the night of the murder, but he dutifully conceded that this point was "very vague."

Bemused by the complexities and ambiguities of the case, Inspector Receveur summarized his tentative theories in a report to his superiors. He had arrived at the belief, he wrote, that it was not professional thieves who killed Leclair, and he was prepared to find the perpetrator of the crime among envious men or among those who would inherit from the victim. The nephew seemed to merit attention, and he was "prepared to look into him deeply." Vial, he noted, was "well advanced in the good graces of the widow," a fact that authorized him to extend his investigation to her as well. The canny Receveur had conceived a new means of reconciling the disappearance of the watch with the theory of Vial's guilt; it was possible that the watch had been stolen by Bourgeois, the gardener, or one of the others who were among the first group to discover the body.

Despite Receveur's suspicion of a conspiracy between Vial and Mme Leclair, the police archives do not indicate that an intensive investigation was made into the widow's possible involvement in the crime. Her deposition was taken, but the questioning appears to have been superficial and pretty much limited to the circumstances under which she learned of her husband's murder. Perhaps it is not unfair to read in her testimony an exaggerated effort to put herself at a safe distance from the crime. She stated that she did not learn of the murder until the afternoon of October 23, even though Paysant had brought the news to her apartment in the morning and had alerted Mlle Petitbois. Mme Leclair did not accompany her god-daughter to Leclair's house, and although it is conceivable that she was not at home that morning, the police records do not indicate that she ever paid a visit thereafter to the scene of the crime.

The investigation into Leclair's death was eventually closed without anyone being charged with the crime. Leclair's devoted memorialist Durosoy had to content himself with inveighing against the unknown murderer: "There are no doubt monsters who do not belong to their country or their age. Such beings have nothing human about them except the face of a man."

The detailed police records that survive provide some basis for hazarding an opinion as to the identity of the guilty party. Was it the gardener Paysant? It hardly seems likely. There is no apparent motive, although a secret grievance of an employee cannot be ruled out. But Paysant seems unfit for the role of murderer. He appears to have been one of those maddeningly unstable witnesses, in love with mystification for its own sake, with whom the annals of French crime have abounded from the Fualdès case of 1817 to the mysterious murder of "little Gregory."

Mme Leclair, the estranged wife of the composer, is the choice of Nicolas Slonimsky. Though she seems to have had little to gain financially from her husband's death—their community property was heavily burdened with debts to a butcher, a wine merchant, a grocer, a mason, and others—we cannot ignore Dorothy Sayers's adage that in a murder case marriage itself can be a motive. Slonimsky, in placing the blame on Mme Leclair, notes that "the three wounds . . . inflicted in the front part of Leclair's body as he faced his murderer . . . might have been caused by a sharp tool used for music engraving—yet there was no examination of these tools in Madame Leclair's apartment in Paris." He also observes that only a person "intimately acquainted with the victim's mode of life" could have gone through the motions of placing the odd group of objects around the corpse and that such a person could only have been Mme Leclair.

Slonimsky, like a good detective-story writer, makes up in strength of assertion for what he lacks in logic. Given the evidence of the violence of Leclair's resistance, it is unlikely that he could have been overwhelmed by a female assailant of advancing years. It also seems possible that Leclair, in wearing a hunting knife at home, may have had reason to fear an enemy more formidable than his wife; he may, in fact, have drawn the knife in his own defense, only to have been overpowered. Moreover, it is not true that only Mme Leclair had sufficient knowledge of Leclair's household to assemble the hat, wig, book, and manuscript paper. Another such person is my candidate for the murderer, the composer's nephew Vial. We cannot determine the cause of estrangement of the Leclairs or the widow's feelings toward her husband; we only know that she claimed to be continuing to supply him with funds in his last days. However, there is no doubt of the depth of Vial's malice or of his irrational conviction that his uncle stood in the way of his musical advancement. He would have known where to find Leclair's manuscript paper (assuming that Leclair, still passionately engaged in composition to the end of his life, did not have the paper at hand when his murderer called), and presumably Vial could have located the joke book in Leclair's library shelves. If the mise-en-scène near the vestibule door contained an ironic message from the murderer, it would have accorded with Vial's bitter spirit for him to have said, through the empty manuscript page, that he had brought the career of his fancied rival to an end and to have sneered, through the title of the joke book, that he had had the last laugh.

Of course, it is possible that Mme Leclair egged Vial on. It is all too apparent that she did not mourn her late husband or grieve the abrupt end of his glorious career. Shortly after his murder, she applied to the police for permission to take an inventory of the contents of his house on rue de Carême-Prenant. On October 26 and 27, 1764, the sale of Leclair's property was carried out and produced less than 2,000 livres, which was insufficient to pay the creditors in full. The following January Leclair's widow sold her husband's violins.

Bibliographical Notes

The principal source for biographical facts and the account of the crime regarding Jean-Marie Leclair (called the "elder" to distinguish him from a younger brother of the same name), and which contains Barnabé Farmian Durosoy's work, is Lionel de la Laurencie, *L'Ecole française de violon de Lully à Viotti*, 3 vols. (Paris: Delagrange, 1922–24), 1:269–349 (Quotations on pp. 298, 302–3).

The records of the investigation of the Paris police into the murder of Leclair, on which this article is based, are located in Archives Nationales (Paris) Y13773 and Archives de la Bastille (Paris) 10068. These archives consist primarily of depositions of witnesses and Inspector Receveur's summary of evidence.

Nicolas Slonimsky's alternative solution to the Leclair mystery is contained in his collection of informal essays on musical subjects, *A Thing or Two about Music* (New York: Allen, Towne and Heath, 1948), 86–90.

The Leclair murder is the subject of a mystery novel by Gérard Gefen, *L'Assassinat de Jean-Marie Leclair* (Paris: Belfond, 1991).

4

Carlo Gesualdo: Murder and Madrigals

Igor Stravinsky has pointed out that Don Carlo Gesualdo, Prince of Venosa (1566–1613), may not have been the first murderer among composers of the Italian Renaissance. In 1570 Massimo Troiano, a poet, singer, and composer, was suspected of involvement, together with another singer, in the murder of a string player, Battista Romano, near Munich. Troiano and the other singer sought by the authorities fled Bavaria to avoid arrest.

On April 27, 1570, Prince Wilhelm of Bavaria wrote (in Latin) to Duke Alfonso of Ferrara, Modena, and Reggio soliciting his aid in apprehending the wanted men: "Two days ago two of our musicians, one Camillo of Parma, the other Massimo Troiano of Naples, who a little before, for no significant cause, conceived hatred against another musician of ours who was outstanding in his art, Battista Romano; and having followed him outside the walls of the town of Landeshut where we are accustomed to reside, suddenly caught sight of him. Each of them fired his weapon at him and one of them lethally wounded the poor fellow." Prince Wilhelm asked Duke Alfonso to do his best to arrest the malefactors, whose descriptions were attached to the letter. Troiano was identified as of middle height with a short reddish beard and speaking in Neapolitan dialect; in "all his words and manners he showed arrogance and haughtiness." Since Troiano never reappeared, his culpability cannot be determined with assurance. However, even if Gesualdo should be regarded as having been second to enter Italian music's murder annals, he far surpassed his predecessor in fame as musician and murderer.

The Gesualdo tragedy was the appalling outcome of a falsely glittering marriage. On the death of his elder brother Luigi in 1585, Carlo, second of two sons, became heir to the Gesualdo family's titles and properties. To ensure the continuity of his line, Carlo's father, Fabrizio, arranged a wedding the following year between Carlo and his twice-widowed first cousin, Donna Maria d'Avalos. Both spouses could boast distinguished ancestry. The Norman noblemen of Gesualdo (taking the family name from a village east of Naples) traced from the eleventh century; Don Carlo's mother, Girolama Borromeo, was a sister of Carlo Borromeo (who became a cardinal in 1560 and was canonized in 1610) and a niece of Pope Pius IV. Donna Maria's father was Don Carlo d'Avalos, Prince of Montesarchio, and her mother was Donna Sveva Gesualdo, her bridegroom's aunt. Donna Maria's two previous husbands, whom she had wed in 1575 and 1580, respectively, were Federigo Carafa, Marchese of San Lucido (with whom she had two children, one surviving only a few months after his birth), and a Sicilian, Alfonso Gioeni, son of the Marchese di Giulianova. An insensitive chronicler speculated that Carafa's early death was perhaps due to excessive indulgence in sexual intercourse with his wife. Musicologist Cecil Gray writes of Donna Maria, who was only twenty-five when she embarked on her third and final marriage: "All contemporary chronicles are agreed on one point, namely, the 'surprising beauty' of Donna Maria, one of them even going so far as to say that she was reputed to be the most beautiful woman in the kingdom of the Two Sicilies. This may seem to us somewhat excessive praise if the portrait of her in the picture . . . of the Carafa family in the church of San Domenico Maggiore at Naples is at all like her."

The first few years of the marriage between Don Carlo and Donna Maria seemed successful, at least from the viewpoint of the Gesualdo family patriarch, because the grandson for whom he had hoped and planned, Emmanuele, was born. Before long, however, the marriage turned a dangerous corner. The events that led Carlo and Maria to catastrophe are chronicled in an early Italian account, known as the Corona Manuscript, which, in its most complete form, has been translated into English by Glenn Watkins in his *Gesualdo: The Man and His Music*. The authors of the manuscript place the blame for the tragedy squarely on uncontrolled female desire: "How much ruin lust has brought to the world is evident for the pages of writers are filled with it, and there is no doubt whatsoever that it brings along with it all sorts of evils and discords, and weakens the body and does harm to all virtues and goodness of the soul. . . . It is lust for which men debase themselves in order to submit the body and soul to the inconstant will and unbridled desire of an unbalanced and vain woman." The marriage of Don Carlo and Maria, according to the narrative, was happy for three or four years, but "the enemy of human nature not being able to endure the sight of such great love and such conformity of tastes in two married people, implanted in the bosom of Donna Maria unchaste and libidinous desires, and an unbridled appetite to enjoy the beauties" of Don Fabrizio Carafa, Duke of Andria, "perhaps the most handsome and graceful cavaliere in the city."

Not only is Maria condemned for the initiation of the torrid affair that followed, but she is held responsible for overruling the duke's proposal to break off their relations when there was reason to know that their secret was out. "My Lord Duke," she supposedly told him, "more deadly to me is a moment when you are away from me than a thousand deaths that might result from my crime."

It proved dangerous for the lovers to wish for disaster. Don Carlo Gesualdo, intent on revenge after his uncle Giulio, himself besotted with Maria, informed him of the adultery, laid his murder plans. "With great speed [he] had all the locks of all the doors of [the Palazzo San Severo, his Naples residence] removed and put out of working order so that [Maria] should not suspect anything" and "spread the news one day that he was going to go hunting . . . and would not return until the following day." Instead, he came back home toward midnight, October 16, 1590, "accompanied [by] a troop of armed cavalieri." After routing a maid who was on watch nearby, he broke down the door of Maria's bedroom and surprised his wife "lying naked in bed in the arms of the Duke."

Even at the sanguinary culmination of their tale, the chroniclers' sympathies for Carlo, the "poor Prince," are unflagging: "At such a sight one can well imagine how dumbfounded the poor Prince was, who, nevertheless, shaking himself loose from the stunned state which such a scene had precipitated in him, slew the sleepy lovers with many dagger thrusts before they could catch their breath." Without reproof to Gesualdo's inhumanity, the Corona Narrative ends by swiftly piling horror upon horror. The bodies were dragged outside the bedroom and left on the stairs, naked to the public gaze. After ordering his servants not to move them and to attach to the palace door "a placard which explained the cause of the slaughters," Carlo departed with some relatives for his principality of Venosa.

The bodies remained on display "all the following morning . . . and the entire city ran thither to view such a spectacle. The Princess's wounds were all in her belly and especially in those parts which most ought to be kept honest; and the Duke gave evidence of having been even more grievously wounded than she." The Corona authors draw a concluding moral that echoes their story's beginning by censuring only the victims: "Such was the end of their unchaste love."

Fuller and more reliable information about the murders is provided in records of three statements of witnesses preserved in records of the investigation undertaken by the Grand Court of the Vicaria on October 27, 1590, in Don Carlo's Naples residence. The statements, which have been translated by Glenn Watkins in his biography of Gesualdo, are those of Dominico Micene, Master of the Court, reporting for himself as well as for two royal councillors and criminal judges of the court and the court's prosecuting attorney; Silvia Albana, Donna Maria's twenty-year-old maid; and Pietro Malitiale, alias Pietro Bardotti, Don Carlo's valet.

Micene's description of the murder scene revealed the multiplicity and brutality of the killers' attacks. The Duke of Andria's body, stretched out on the floor and bizarrely clad in a "woman's nightdress with fringes at the bottom, with ruffs of black silk," was covered with blood and pierced with many wounds: "an arquebusade on his left arm which went straight through his elbow, and even went through his breast, the sleeve of the above-mentioned shirt being scorched; signs of diverse wounds made by pointed steel weapons on the breast, arms, on the head and on the face; and another arquebus wound in his temples and over his eye where there was a great flow of blood." Donna Maria's body lay on a gilt couch with bed curtains of green cloth; she "was in her nightshirt all bathed in blood." Her throat had been cut, and there were "also a wound on the head on the side of her right temple, a stab on the face and a number of dagger thrusts on her hand and right arm, and on her breast and side there was evidence of two other wounds inflicted by weapons."

Confirming certain puzzling details of the Corona Narrative, the statement of the court master Micene reports that "in the quarter of [Donna Maria's] apartment," the door "was found to be smashed at the bottom and could not be shut with the handle in view of the fact that the keyhole was so gouged out that it could not be shut, nor could one secure the door nor the lock of said door." If the door could not be shut or locked, why would intruders have smashed the bottom of the door, except in rage? An additional issue is raised by the damage to the door in advance of the crimes: the conspirators' tinkering with the keyhole and lock, apparently in order to ease surreptitious entry on the murder night, might have alerted the lovers to imminent danger.

The two domestic servants who gave evidence to the court investigators substantiated the active role of Don Carlo in the murders. Silvia Albana testified that on the night of the murders she and another servant, Laura Scala, put Donna Maria to bed as usual. After a while her mistress told her she wished to dress, explaining that she had heard the Duke of Andria whistle and wished to go to the window, as Silvia had seen her do many times. Donna Maria, having dressed and gone out on the balcony, instructed the witness to stand guard. A half hour later, Donna Maria closed the window and told the maid to undress her once again. She also ordered her to bring her a fresh nightshirt because the one she was wearing was wet with perspiration; the nightshirt that Silvia brought her mistress was the same garment that the witness had seen the Duke of Andria wearing when she later discovered him in Donna Maria's bedroom, dead on the floor. Her lady's last instruction was to "shut the door without turning the handle and do not come in unless I call you." She had decided not to undress after all and fell asleep reading a book. Later that night the maid was awakened by a sound on the spiral staircase that led to a mezzanine where Don Carlo had his quarters. She saw three men enter whom she did not recognize. They opened the door to her mistress's bedroom, and she saw that "one of them, who was the last of the three, was carrying a halberd." The witness then heard two shots and almost simultaneously the words "There he is!" Nearly at the same time she saw Don Carlo enter the bedroom by the staircase attended by his valet, Pietro Bardotti, carrying two lighted torches. Don Carlo was carrying a halberd and thundered, "Ah, traitress, I shall kill you. You shall not escape me now!" The witness fled into a room "where the boy child was," and from there she heard Don Carlo saying in her mistress's bedroom, "Where are they?" The maid begged that "for the love of God he should not hurt the child." Don Carlo ordered his valet to close the door of the closet where his wife kept her jewels and then departed. When she asked her fellow servant what had happened, Bardotti replied, "Both of them are dead!" Watkins interprets Silvia's testimony as suggesting that "Gesualdo's helpers, while entering first, disposed of the Duke of Andria and left the Princess to Don Carlo."

The valet, Pietro Bardotti, about forty years old, told investigators that he had served his master and his house for twenty-eight years. On the murder night Don Carlo called him to ask for a drink of water. After returning from the well, he saw that Don Carlo was dressed. When the witness asked where he was going at such a late hour, his master replied that he wanted to go hunting. When Bardotti expressed surprise, Don Carlo answered, "You will see the kind of hunting I am going to do!" After Bardotti lighted two torches as instructed, "Don Carlo took from under the bed a sword and gave it to the witness to carry under his arm, also a dirk and a dagger together with a small arquebus." As the two men went to the staircase that led to Donna Maria's apartment, Don Carlo said, "I am going to slay the Duke of Andria and that whore, Donna Maria." As Don Carlo was going up, Bardotti saw three men, each of whom was carrying a halberd and a small arquebus. When the witness arrived, the men threw open Donna Maria's door. As they entered the bedroom, Don Carlo said, "Kill that scoundrel along with this harlot! Shall a Gesualdo be made a cuckold?" The witness then heard the sound of firearms but could not distinguish any voices because he stayed outside. When Don Carlo's henchmen came out, Bardotti recognized "one to be Pietro de Vicario, a servant, another as Ascanio Lama, and a third as a servant whose name was Francesco." They descended by the same staircase by which they had come. When Don Carlo emerged, his hands covered with blood, he had a sudden qualm that compelled him to reenter the bedroom, saying, "I do not believe they are dead!" Bardotti followed him with a torch and saw the duke's dead body near the door. As he looked on, Don Carlo went up to Donna Maria's bed and "inflicted still a few more wounds upon her saying, 'I do not believe she is dead.'"

Watkins relates that immediately after the murders Don Carlo consulted the Spanish viceroy of Naples, Don Giovanni Zunia of Miranda, seeking his advice as to the best course of action, and also razed the forest that surrounded his castle in Gesualdo to prevent possible enemies from lying in wait. It is not clear that the viceroy took any official action in the murder investigation. Cecil Gray comments, "The copyist of the document adds that the inquiry was discontinued at the command of the Viceroy, in view of the manifest justification for the Prince's act in slaying the Duke of Andria and his own erring spouse. But this would seem merely to be a personal opinion of the scribe."

There is strong evidence that the violence and unhinged emotion in Gesualdo's life did not end with the murders in his Naples residence.

Left: Don Carlo Gesualdo. A detail of a painting in the chapel of Santa Maria delle Grazie, Gesualdo, Italy. Right: Don Carlo's ill-fated first wife, Donna Maria d'Avalos. A detail of the painting of the Carafa family in the church of San Domenico Maggiore, Naples, Italy.

However, biographer Glenn Watkins justifiably dismisses as incredible a rumor that Gesualdo also murdered a second son, who would have been only a few months old. The rumor claimed that "Gesualdo believed that he recognized in the presumed child certain features of the Duke of Andria. His mind having been thus poisoned, he soon reached a state of mental frenzy, had the infant 'put in a cradle in the large hall of his castle, and suspended it with cords of silk hanging down from two nails which were hammered into the arch. He then ordered that the crib be subjected to wild undulations, until through the violence of the motion, not being able to draw breath, the child rendered up its soul to God.'" Watkins notes that there is no surviving record of the birth of a second Gesualdo son.

Far from desiring to add to the sum of his murders, Gesualdo by 1592 was in a mood for atonement. In that year he completed the building of a Capuchin monastery at Gesualdo, with a chapel named S. Maria delle Grazie. Glenn Watkins describes a painting in the chapel that appears to represent divine forgiveness for Gesualdo's killings: "At the top of the picture in the centre the Redeemer sits in judgement. The Prince [Gesualdo] appears in the lower left-hand corner in a kneeling position dressed in the Spanish fashion, while Saint Carlo Borromeo, Archbishop of Milan and his maternal uncle, 'attired in his Cardinal's robes, places his right arm protectively on his erring nephew's shoulder, with his face turned towards the Divine Redeemer in the act of presenting him.'"

In spite of his search for religious comfort, Gesualdo's personal life remained in wild disorder. In the years after a politically inspired marriage to Donna Leonora d'Este of Ferrara in 1594, his repeated beating and abuse of her brought the couple close to divorce. Symptoms of masochism were also the subject of comment in Don Ferrante della Marra's 1632 chronicle, *Rovine di Case Napolitane del suo tempo (Ruins of Neapolitan Houses of His Time):* "The third misfortune was that through the agency of God, [Gesualdo] was assailed and afflicted by a vast horde of demons which gave him no peace for many days on end unless ten or twelve young men, whom he kept specially for the purpose, were to beat him violently three times a day, during which operation he was wont to smile joyfully." A medical treatise of 1635 offered an alternative report that the Prince of Venosa was flogged by a valet to relieve his chronic constipation.

For more than four hundred years, the Gesualdo murder case has evoked responses in diverse genres of literature. The preeminent poet Torquato Tasso (1544–1595), a friend of the killer and his victims, met Gesualdo in 1588, perhaps at the *camerata,* or academy, that the Prince sponsored at his Naples residence. Invitations to the camerata assembled composers, musical performers, and poets. During the years of these gatherings, Gesualdo, according to musicologist Cecil Gray, learned composition and received instruction in the playing of several instruments, including the bass-lute. From 1592 on, Tasso, a leading exponent of madrigal poetry, sent Gesualdo more than forty madrigals to be set to music, and at least fourteen have been identified as having made their way into the prince's published compositions. The five-voice madrigal became Gesualdo's principal musical form.

The double murder did not interrupt Tasso's friendship for Gesualdo, but in four sonnets he poured out his grief over the deaths of Donna Maria and the Duke of Andria. In one of his poems, "On the Death of Two Most Noble Lovers" (as translated by Glenn Watkins), no palliation is offered for the "horrible event" that took the lives of "two most noble lovers":

Weep, O Graces, and you too bewail, O Loves, the cruel trophies of death and the cruel spoils of the beautiful couple whom death enviously takes from us, both the funeral pomps and the shadowy horrors.

Weep, O Nymphs, and strew blossoms on this couple, their moist leaves painted with old lamentations; and all you who vie with each other in distilling the piteous anguish and the scent of tears.

Other poets, some distinguished and others anonymous, also memorialized the dead lovers.

The story of Donna Maria and her lover was told by Gesualdo's contemporary, Pierre de Bourdeilles, Seigneur and Abbé Brantôme (ca. 1540–1614), in his *Lives of Fair and Gallant Ladies*. Brantôme apparently did not believe that Don Carlo personally took part in the slaughter of the lovers, but his book related the legend that the morning after the murder "the fair and noble pair, unhappy beings, were seen lying stretched out and exposed to public view on the pavement in front of the house door, all dead and cold, in sight of all passers-by, who could not but weep and lament over their piteous lot." The lady's relatives were hot to avenge her killing "by death and murder as the law of [Naples] doth allow," but the focus of their anger struck Brantôme as distinctly odd. They would not have sought satisfaction from Gesualdo if he had struck the blows with his own hands. What Donna Maria's family resented was that the prince had had his wife slain by "base-born varlets and slaves who deserved not to have their hands stained with so good and noble blood." The outraged relatives felt that this point alone should be the ground for their seeking satisfaction from Don Carlo "whether by justice or otherwise." Brantôme regarded this position as a foolish quibble: "I make appeal to our great orators and wise lawyers that they tell me this: which act is the more monstrous, for a man to kill his wife with his own hand, the which hath so oftentimes loved and caressed her, or by that of a base-born slave?"

The names of two characters in John Ford's tragedy *Love's Sacrifice* (1633) clearly identify the Gesualdo murder case as a real-life source of the work: Philippo Caraffa, Duke of Pavia, and his secretary, Roderico d'Avolos, respectively bear, in variant spellings, the surname of Donna Maria's first husband and of her lover and her own family name. The drama's plot, like the adultery in the Gesualdo household, leads inexorably to multiple deaths caused by a husband's jealousy. The Duke of Pavia has wed Bianca, a young Milanese beauty who refers to herself as a "simple gentlewoman." Bianca falls in love with the Duke's favorite, Fernando, but spurns his repeated advances. At last, slipping into his bedchamber, she confesses a reciprocating passion that may be even stronger than his own:

Since first mine eyes beheld you, in my heart
You have been only king. If there can be

A violence in love, then I have felt
That tyranny.

Because of Fernando's loyalty to the Duke, the young couple express their love only by the exchange of chaste kisses.

While this romance blossoms, two dangerous conspirators are waiting for the strategic moment to inform the duke: Fiormonda, the duke's sister, and Roderico d'Avolos, an ambitious courtier. When d'Avolos persuades the duke that Bianca has cuckolded him, the enraged husband pretends to leave on a journey to Lucca but returns to confront his wife in her bedchamber. Although denying infidelity, Bianca, more bravely than wisely, explains her preference for Fernando. You married me, she tells her husband, "because you thought I had / a spark of beauty more than you had seen." Her reason for loving Fernando was the same:

The selfsame appetite which led you on
To marry me, led me to love your friend.
O he's a gallant man.

Her husband stabs her to death with a dagger. Fernando takes poison, and the duke, in remorse after learning of his wife's innocence, "sacrifices his life" on her altar.

In his short story "History of Doña Maria d'Avalos and Don Fabricio, Duke d'Andria," Anatole France (1844–1924) pursued the narrative tradition of the Corona Manuscript and of Brantôme. Unlike the Corona version of the underlying events, France's retelling invites sympathy for Maria's youthful inexperience and her prefigured surrender to the overwhelming power of love. To emphasize her innocence, France omits any reference to Maria's previous marriages. He forecasts her doom by describing a *tableau vivant* on a cart in her wedding procession that features a "winged youth treading underfoot three old hags of incredible ugliness"; a sign above the vehicle proclaimed that "Love Vanquishes the Fatal Sisters." By this deceptive maxim "'twas to be understood that the new-wedded pair would enjoy many a long year of happiness by each other's side," but "this presage of Love, more strong than the Fates, was false withal."

When Maria saw the Duke d'Andria, she found him "a gallant, handsome and well-knit man, and did straight love the same. An honest girl and a well-born, heedful of her noble name and still in that callow youth when women have not gotten boldness yet to match their naughty desires, she sent no go-between to the nobleman to make assignation in Church or in her own abode." She bided her time and did not have to wait long. The Duke "had noted her beauty," declared his love and she responded, refusing him "naught of all he was fain to have of her."

France adopts the Corona episode in which Maria rebuffs the duke's attempt to break off their affair, and the bloody denouement swiftly follows. In his adaptation, six men take part in the murders, "led on by the Prince, being of his bosom friends every one or his own varlets." The prince taunts Maria by pricking her belly with the point of his sword and, maddened with jealousy when she throws herself on the duke's bleeding corpse, drives his blade through her body. At the end of his tale, France spares his readers none of the indignities reported by the Corona Manuscript to have been inflicted on the victims' bodies.

Alberto Consiglio's historical novel about the Gesualdo murders, *Gesualdo: or, Murder in Five Voices,* rejects the tradition that Donna Maria was oversexed, a "devourer of men" who had worn out two husbands. He portrays her, instead, as suffering a feeling of exclusion from locked recesses in her husband's personality: "The desperation of Maria was not carnal. Her torment was not jealousy, even of an immaterialized woman, or of an incorporeal image, Music, Carlo's real woman. Maria mortified herself in shame. In that absence of her husband, in his partial and occasional participation in conjugal love, in that love of his with its wide reserves, she felt prostituted, she felt like a cleaning rag, and she seemed to bear in her breast the vivid and painful marks of the cuirasses with which mercenary soldiers had pressed against her."

For Don Fabrizio, Duke of Andria, as depicted by Consiglio, the love affair with Donna Maria fills the void of an unempowered life. His household is dominated by Jesuits; his wife and three of his four children are extremely devout. The hypochondriacal duke, as the member of a powerful Neapolitan family, is excluded from a career in military or public service by the Spanish viceroy, who pretends to seek his advice on matters of policy. Fabrizio leads an expedition against brigands, but even this adventure proves illusory; he and his men kill more wild boars than bandits.

On his return to Naples, he hears scurrilous rumors about Donna Maria and her relations with Don Giulio Gesualdo, her husband's uncle, whose advances she has in fact rejected. These stories whet the Duke of Andria's interest in the scandalous Maria, and he is delighted to have an opportunity to meet her at the viceroy's ball, particularly since his stern wife has refused to attend. At the party the young couple fall in love as they dance, while the viceroy looks on in horror.

The romance that follows is brought to the attention of Maria's husband by his jealous uncle, Don Giulio. Gesualdo sets a death trap after learning from his valet Bardotti that Donna Maria's pet gyrfalcon "has escaped." Gesualdo thinks quickly: "Why did Maria have a gyrfalcon? Who gave it to her? He remembered vaguely the story that they had passed on to him of a merchant from Barbary who had sold [the bird] to Laura [his wife's maid] for thirty ducats." The prince concluded rightly that his wife had dispatched the messenger bird to summon her lover. Don Carlo's mental agility is stirred further when he observes his wife's radiant face over the dinner table: "The great misfortune of that tragic story was the presence in it of a poet, of a man of imagination. Was the happiness of Maria the lightning that illumined Carlo's mind? In a moment, the husband saw everything. The gyrfalcon was a gift of Carafa [the Duke of Andria]. She had sent the bird that night so that it could carry her desperate message. . . . At that point, he decided to reorganize his death trap for the following Tuesday."

Consiglio's account of the murders incorporates the three depositions included in the records of the investigation. The novelist, however, adds his own explanation for the discovery of the duke's body clad in Donna Anna's nightgown. Her lover had arrived covered in dust and mud and bathed in sweat. "Maria had maternally foreseen this; she dried his back and chest and made him put on the gown that Silvia had prepared."

In the final chapter the viceroy has the court record read to him. After hearing the recitation, he finds premeditation on both sides—that of the husband and that of the two lovers. "They knew everything about the trap laid by Gesualdo, and entered there like two spouses into church, like two of the dying into their tomb." He writes to King Philip of Spain to "inform him in detail and to explain the grave reasons of State that counseled impunity for the Prince of Venosa, Don Carlo Gesualdo, nephew of two Cardinals of the Holy Roman Church, and his accomplices."

The Gesualdo murders have been the subject of two crime studies, an essay by musicologist Cecil Gray in the style of Thomas De Quincey and a psychological exploration by Shlomo Giora Shoham. Both the title of Gray's essay, "Carlo Gesualdo Considered as a Murderer," and its mock-aestheticism reflect Thomas De Quincey's famous articles of 1827 and 1839, "On Murder

Considered as One of the Fine Arts." In view of the butchery for which Gesualdo was responsible, it was an unfortunate lapse of taste that led Gray to adopt the satiric manner of these essays; a more appropriate tone could have been borrowed from De Quincey's 1854 supplement, "Three Memorable Murders," in which the author turned from humor to suspenseful and psychologically acute crime narratives. Nevertheless, when the distractions of literary parody are overcome, it is possible to perceive the lines of Gray's crime analysis. He maintains that, "contrary to expectations, Gesualdo was not . . . in position, despite his exalted rank . . . to kill anyone who happens to annoy [him] with absolute impunity." He further observes that "one of the Venetian ambassadors to Naples about this time, Michele Suriano, considered it one of the defects of the viceregal government that affairs of justice were executed without making any distinction between nobles and common people—a defect because punishment means so little to a mere commoner, and so much to a nobleman."

Gray sees Gesualdo's crimes as typical of the late Renaissance—in which "even creative artists, philosophers, and scholars, were not averse to dabbling occasionally in [destruction]"—and he cites many exemplars, including Tasso: "The poet Chiabrera murdered a Roman gentleman in revenge for an insult; the historian Davila also committed a murder and was himself assassinated; Tasso, in his periodic fits of frenzy, was wont to attack people with a dagger." The essay suggests in its conclusion that Gesualdo's life can be compartmentalized, that "it was not until Gesualdo gave up murder that he seriously took up composing."

A chapter entitled "Don Carlo Gesualdo—A Murdered Love" is included in Shoham's *Art, Crime and Madness*. Professor Shoham, who has written on crime, deviance, philosophy, religion, psychology, and the human personality, constructs an unflattering image of Gesualdo's psyche: "Don Carlo's personality was presumably doubly fixated, both at the early and later oral stages of development, so that a 'black hole' was structured within it. Gesualdo tried to 'fill' this abyss by unrequited love, both sadistic and masochistic, and after he murdered his wife, by guilt and self-inflicted pain." Shoham finds support for his conception of Gesualdo's sadomasochistic nature not only in the composer's addiction to being flogged but also in his fondness for madrigal lyrics associating love with physical pain. He cites, for example, a Tasso lyric for a Gesualdo madrigal in which love causes a painless array of torments to assail the heart:

O Love, my blessed one,
I feel without pain
another dart, other chains,
another flame.

In Shoham's vision, the composer's music reflects his guilt over the murder of Donna Maria: "Gesualdo's wish to join his beloved wife [Maria] in death" is "linked to his magnificently expressionist and tortured music."

It is a risky venture, of course, to seek reflections of Gesualdo's violent impulses in the music he composed years after his double murder. Gesualdo's musical style became adventurous only gradually; Glenn Watkins observes that Gesualdo's early madrigals reveal "a composer well versed in the traditions of contrapuntal practice" and refers to "the greater harmonic orientation of many of his later works." Only as the murders receded in his past did Gesualdo become a musical innovator. If a search for violence in his music will baffle us, still less confidently can we read Gesualdo's psyche in the lyrics of others he chose to set in his madrigals. The pains of lost or spurned love were the stock in trade of madrigal poets.

Bibliographical Notes

The Latin letter from Prince Wilhelm about Massimo Troiano's involvement in murder is published in the article "Massimo Trojano als Flüchtling [Massimo Trojano as a Fugitive]," *Monatshefte für Musikgeschichte* 23, 1 (1891): 1–4. The weapons used were apparently a stonebow (*parvum tormentum*) and a firearm (*bombarda*).

The most complete Italian edition of the so-called Corona Manuscript relating the Gesualdo murder case is editor Angelo Borzelli's *Successi Tragici et Amorosi di Silvio et Ascanio Corona* [Cases of Tragedy and Love by Silvio and Ascanio Corona] (Naples: Casella, 1908), 192–203. Existing variants of this manuscript date from the late seventeenth or early eighteenth century. Borzelli believes that many authors had a hand in this work and that Corona was their common pseudonym. English translations of the Corona Manuscript and of the police investigation into the Gesualdo murders are found in both the Cecil and Heseltine and the Watkins biographies cited below.

Biographical studies of Gesualdo include Cecil Gray's essay "Carlo Gesualdo Considered as a Murderer," found in *Carlo Gesualdo Prince of Venosa Musician and Murderer* (London: Kegan Paul, 1926), which he coauthored with Philip Heseltine (Gray's murder essay at pp. 61–74); Denis Mortier, *Carlo Gesualdo* (Paris: Fayard,

2003); Shlomo Giora Shoham, *Art, Crime and Madness* (Brighton, England: Sussex Academic Press, 2002), 73–93; and Glenn P. Watkins, *Gesualdo: The Man and His Music,* with a preface by Igor Stravinsky, 2nd ed. (Oxford, England: Oxford Univ. Press, 1991), 3–91 (biography), 6–23 (Corona Manuscript and murders), 32 (portrayal of G. in the chapel of Santa Maria delle Grazie), 33–34 (infanticide rumor), 73–81 (G.'s mistreatment of second wife), 83 (masochism of G. and its report in *Rovine di Case Napolitane del suo tempo*).

A novel based on the Gesualdo murders is Michel Breitman's *LeTémoin de Poussière* [The Witness of Dust] (Paris: Robert Laffont, 1985), in which Gesualdo's devoted servant, Gioseppe Pilonij, narrates his master's rise and tragedy resulting from two murder plots: a faked hunting accident claiming the life of Gesualdo's elder brother, Luigi, and the massacre of Maria d'Avalos and her lover. In reality Pilonij was a Neapolitan under whose name Gesualdo published his early madrigals.

Other works of fiction include include a collection of scandalous anecdotes by [Pierre de Bourdeilles] Seigneur and Abbé de Brantôme, *Fair and Gallant Ladies,* trans. A. R. Allinson (New York: Liveright, 1933); Alberto Consiglio's novel *Gesualdo ovvero Assassinio a Cinque Voci* [Gesualdo: or, Murder in Five Voices] (Naples: Berisio, 1967); John Ford's play *Love's Sacrifice,* ed. A. T. Moore (Manchester: Manchester Univ. Press, Revels Plays, 2002); Anatole France's "History of Dona Maria d'Avalos and the Duke d'Andria," in *The Well of Saint Clare,* trans. Alfred Allinson (London: John Lane, Bodley Head, 1909), 271–86; and Jean-Noël Schifano's novella *Madrigal napolitain,* in *Chroniques napolitaines* (Paris: Gallimard, 1984).

The murders of Donna Maria and her lover have inspired two operas entitled *Gesualdo,* one by Alfred Schnittke (premiered in Vienna, May 26, 1995) and the other by Franz Hummel (first produced in Kaiserslautern, Germany, in 1996). Director Werner Herzog's self-indulgent 1995 film for television, a so-called "documentary fiction" called "Death for Five Voices," has no relation to the similarly named novel by Alberto Consiglio. The Herzog film is available on DVD, distributed by Image Entertainment.

5

Alessandro Stradella: Revenge for Love

A French history of music begun by Abbé Pierre Bourdelot and completed and published in 1715 by his nephew Jacques Bonnet established the myth that long surrounded the first attempt to murder Alessandro Stradella (1639–1682). According to this tantalizing story, a Venetian nobleman engaged composer Stradella to give music lessons to his mistress. Stradella eloped with his pupil to Rome, pursued by two assassins hired by his vengeful employer. On arrival in the Eternal City, the *bravi* learned that the faithless Stradella was to perform a new oratorio on the next day at the Basilica of San Giovanni in Laterano, one of Rome's four patriarchal churches. The murderous pair planned to attack the composer when he left the church, but they were so strongly moved by the beauty of his music that they could not bring themselves to strike. Instead, they implored Stradella to save his life by leaving Rome immediately.

The Stradella legend is so romantic that, according to Stradella's biographer Carolyn Gianturco, it inspired six nineteenth-century operas of which the best known is *Alessandro Stradella* (1837) by Friedrich von Flotow. In Flotow's comic opera, Stradella's music softens the hearts of his would-be killers and of the master whom they served. At the end of the second act, the bandits who have entered Stradella's house surreptitiously are diverted from their bloody mission when he sings a ballad of landscape painter Salvator Rosa glorifying the compassion of highwaymen. In the opera finale the vindictive nobleman also recovers his humanity, calling on Stradella to forgive and forget after hearing the composer's rehearsal of a hymn to the Virgin Mary.

Gianturco's *Alessandro Stradella, 1639–1682: His Life and Music* has made the most decisive shift from fiction to fact in treating the biography and career of this significant figure in music history. Stradella, described by Ellen Rosand in her review of Gianturco's book as "an important composer of vocal and instrumental music in Italy during the third quarter of the seventeenth century," produced cantatas, operas and other theater music, oratorios (including one of his finest works, *San Giovanni Battista*), vocal pieces, madrigals, and instrumental music. He is credited with inventing the concerto grosso.

The birthplace of Stradella was the city of Nepi, near Viterbo in central Italy. His father, Marc'Antonio, was, according to Gianturco, "one of the leading figures of Nepi," and the family was well-connected with luminaries in aristocratic and church circles. Marc'Antonio died in 1648, and five years later the fourteen-year-old Alessandro moved with his mother, Vittoria, and his brother, Stefano, to Rome; Vittoria joined Duke Ippolito Lante's household, which her two sons served as pages. The details of Alessandro's musical training are obscure, but in 1667 a Latin oratorio of his was performed during the Lenten season in a series paid for by a society of aristocrats. Throughout his productive life, Stradella served many patrons. A particularly loyal supporter was a Venetian nobleman, Polo Michiel, and in about 1675 Queen Christina of Sweden (who had taken up residence in Rome after her abdication) made one of her many contributions to his career, writing a scenario that was developed into a verse that Stradella set to music in his cantata *Il Damone*.

The fact that Stradella served numerous masters was a mixed blessing at best. The continuity of his work was not assured, and his noble patrons were not always quick to pay for the music that they had commissioned. These inherent risks of musical freelancing may have been exacerbated by Stradella's high living. Whatever the causes, by the autumn of 1670 the young composer found himself in debt for 7,000 scudi and turned to Cardinal Flavio Chigi for assistance. In a letter of November 27 to the cardinal, Stradella emphasized both his humility and the danger he faced: "I am here with this sheet of paper, prostrate at Your Excellency's feet, kneeling before Your Clemency to beg for help, and to request your magnanity to free me from a disgrace which is hovering above me, [a situation] in which, if I have no protector, I could be deprived of my belongings, reputation, and perhaps also freedom." The root cause of his misery, Stradella submitted, was his professional independence: "Your Excellency should . . . know that it is already two years that I am free-lancing to earn some money, and that so far I have had reasonable good luck; but, whoever navigates this particular sea, and does not have someone to protect him from the abuses of fortune, must succumb to several encounters with the same." Stradella informed the cardinal that to satisfy his needs, a loan of 2,000 scudi would be sufficient because he had already put together the rest. He then attempted to apply time pressure: "The time left to remedy this misfortune is only until the coming Saturday; it is therefore the shortness of the [time] that leads me to disturb Your Excellency. If by any chance you would agree to help me, your money is safe." It is not known whether or how the cardinal responded, but Gianturco suggests that Stradella's plight may have been ameliorated by 1671 when he became active in work for Rome's first public opera theater, the Teatro Tordinona.

Years earlier, however, Stradella had set a dangerous precedent for supplementing his income by disreputable marriage brokering. Gianturco summarizes a 1667 letter from Abate Settimio Olgiati to Polo Michiel informing him that Stradella "has arranged a marriage and, because of it, has had to escape to a religious institution and may even have to leave Rome." A similar affair cropped up nine years later. Stradella makes a veiled reference to this new misstep in his letter of October 20, 1676, to Polo Michiel, where he alludes to "a certain misfortune having happened to me in Rome, which does not permit me to live here at the moment." One account cited by Gianturco asserted that "he contrived to get 10,000 scudi from a woman 'of low birth, not respectable, . . . also ugly and old.'" Another version of the rumor claimed that Stradella and an accomplice, a well-known contralto castrato, tried to cover their tracks by marrying their victim off to a relative of Cardinal Alderano Cibo; supposedly the chosen husband was an unidentified member of the Cibo family. The consequence of this attempted offense against family honor was that the cardinal had the woman put in a nunnery, "one of the most vile" in Rome. Stradella thought it best to decamp for Venice.

No sooner had he arrived there than he became involved in a new imbroglio before which his earlier troubles paled. Alvise Contarini, a member of a rich and powerful Venetian family, asked Stradella to give music lessons to his *inamorata,* Agnese Van Uffele. But by June 1677 the composer no longer had tutorial duties on his mind; he eloped with the young woman to Turin, capital of the Duchy of Savoy. Contarini was furious, railing not over a broken heart but stolen goods; he insisted that the fugitives had robbed him of 10,000 ducats. He was not believed, Gian-turco relates, "since he was talking about jewels of little value which he had given his mistress." The nobleman's anger, if not his financial loss, was real, for in late July he arrived in Turin in search of the lovers; he found that the girl had sought refuge in a convent for "lost sheep" and her lover had claimed sanctuary at the Convent of San Domenico. Through pressure applied by an archbishop, Contarini insisted that Agnese either marry Stradella or become a nun. By the end of the month, Contarini left the city, and Stradella turned to his patron Polo Michiel for intercession. In a letter of August 21, 1677, Stradella asked Michiel for written recommendations to the Turin court.

> The reason why I ask Your Excellency this favour is because Signor Aluigi [Alvise] Contarini having advanced his cause here just by saying that I am a thief, that I robbed him of money, with a thousand other lies, . . . I need letters to this court which testify to my actions. . . . The same Signor Aluigi was nevertheless not believed, and they excused his slander by believing him to be very passionate and in love; but with all that, I have always been open with the court and . . . am always ready to receive every reprimand whenever I have committed by my actions a positive error. As far as the woman is concerned, . . . I did not take her away to remove her from Signor Aluigi, but because of the compassion that I had for the misfortunes of the same, for the dangers in which I saw her, and because of the continuous and innumerable supplications she made me.

On September 11 Stradella wrote again, expressing the hope that Michiel would lend his support in the continuing dispute, since he had "the opportunity of using [his] very powerful contacts with Signor Aluigi Contarini." By the following month, negotiations seemed to be bearing fruit. On October 8 an informant reported to Michiel that Stradella had at last agreed to marry Agnese; in return, Contarini would return the girl's belongings. After the wedding, the nobleman would in writing both pardon Stradella and recommend him to Savoy's regent, Maria Giovanna. The rejoicings of the now affianced couple were, however, premature, as a news bulletin from Turin to Rome soon reported: "Sunday evening [October 10] Alessandro Stradella, *Musico Romano,* was assaulted by two outsiders [*forestieri*], and they dealt him several knife wounds, leaving him on the ground for dead, and being brought into the *Palazzo* of S. Giovanni, orders were immediately given by Madama Reale [Maria Giovanna] to bring him to the rooms he has in the Convent of San Domenico, and therefore a rigorous search is being made to find the emissaries." In fact, the identity of the man who ordered the attack (from which Stradella recovered) was, in the minds of many, an open secret. On October 16 the Bavarian ambassador reported the crime to Munich and named Contarini as responsible. Ultimately, nobody was brought to justice because the case became snarled with diplomatic quarrels between France and Savoy.

Stradella's correspondence with Michiel shows that the victim of the assault was also quick to put the dangerous conflict behind him. He informed Michiel on November 26, 1677, that "every difference that the most excellent Signor Aluigi Contarini had with me is completely settled to my great satisfaction, as well as the way [it was done]," and in a letter of December 16 he further assured his patron: "Your Excellency is already well informed of my peace of mind with regard to the most excellent Signor Contarini."

There is no further mention of Agnese Van Uffele in Stradella's correspondence. This passionate triangle disappears from history only to re-emerge in the happier form of the Bourdelot-Bonnet myth and the Flotow opera. For Stradella, though, destiny proved far harsher than these fictions. Although to all appearances unchastened by his close brush with disaster, he thought it best to move to Genoa, where he was well-settled by January 1668. It was in this city that the composer's reckless nature set him on a course leading to a last misadventure.

From a professional point of view, Stradella's years in Genoa turned out to be brilliantly successful. To keep this musical star in their city, a group of Genoese gave him an annual stipend of 100 Spanish doubloons as well as a house, food, and a servant; he was also entrusted with management of the Teatro Falcone. In Genoa Stradella produced three of his operas, *La forza dell'amore paterno, Le gare dell'amor eroico,* and *Il Trespolo tutore;* another opera was commissioned from Rome and an oratorio, *La Susanna,* was presented in Modena. His pupils burgeoned among the nobility.

In other respects, however, Genoa was far from a perfect location for Stradella. Both the public and private spheres of the city were extremely puritanical. The three ruling doges, as well as the Genoese Senate, closely regulated the social behavior of citizens. Rules of conduct published in 1680 made detailed prescriptions for clothing and adornment, decreeing black for the dress of women and requiring simplicity in jewelry and wigs. The rigor of such ordinances was contagious, arousing the public to emulate the zeal of its government. Gianturco cites an anonymous letter of complaint to the governing council in which an unflattering reference was made to Stradella. The writer found that women were ostentatious and their husbands extravagant. The men, he fulminated, gave too much money to a fashionable hairdresser nicknamed "the Roman" and to two composers, Stradella, and his friend, Carlo Ambrosio Lonati, a hunch-backed singer, violinist, and composer—"they throw money so that these brazen scoundrels can stay in Genoa." The letter concluded that the three offenders should be expelled from the city. Gianturco notes that the thrust of the letter's author was ambiguous, targeting either money or immoral-ity: "He is opposed to women being glamorous and, what is more, suspi-cious of their dealings with men outside the family. . . . He is against all expenditures for things he believes valueless, for example money paid to Stradella and Lonati supposedly for their compositions or music lessons. He would presumably have seen their lessons to ladies as immoral en-counters simply because of the proximity of the sexes."

A spate of anonymous letters beginning on December 2, 1681, com-mented on the recent wounding of Pier Francesco Guano that required twelve stitches on his face. The letters asserted that Guano had been at-tacked for having "talked too loudly and sarcastically especially about having seen nude noblewomen." On February 28, 1682, a news brief sent from Genoa to Florence reported another attack, this one claiming the life of Alessandro Stradella: "Wednesday evening [February 25] at two at night [about 7:00 P.M.] while he was going home accompanied by his ser-vant who had a cape in his hand, the musician Stradella was stabbed three times, and died immediately without being able to say a word, and the servant whom he had ahead [of him] observed nothing until he saw him fall flat on his face, and then he died, and it is not yet known who did it." A composer of admired music, Stradella died in silence. His burial in Santa Maria delle Vigne, one of Genoa's most aristocratic churches, confirmed what his unbroken ties with noble patrons had already demonstrated: pri-vate indiscretions had not dimmed the respect he had enjoyed because of his music and his family ties.

Although the news report of February 28 termed the perpetrator un-known, political and public opinion, expressed anonymously, placed the blame on the four Lomellino brothers. One unsigned note in the records of the investigation suggested that if Stradella "had paid attention to the admonitions he had received in Turin[,] he would not have had such an accident which might have been caused by his wanting to raise his sight to the sun. Therefore whoever rises too high is bound to fall." This implication that Stradella's sin was to pursue love affairs in Genoa's high society was sardonically phrased in musical terms by news reports stating that "in order to touch too high he had played in the bass." Reports also claimed that three other leading musicians had left Genoa so as to avoid Stradella's fate.

On March 5 the Genoese Senate ordered Giovanni Battista Lomellino (known as Bacciolo or Baccio) and his brother Domenico to be imprisoned. A month later the men were released on a payment of 2,000 silver scudi. They were never formally charged with Stradella's murder, nor was sufficient evidence assembled to support such an accusation. Anonymous letters had charged that the killing was arranged because Stradella was having an affair with the accused men's married sister, Maria Lomellino Garibaldi. This imputation may have been no more than an attempt to suggest comparison to Alvise Contarini's commissioned act of revenge in Turin. Apart from the lack of proof, biographer Gianturco finds an additional reason to doubt this theory, finding it "a bit surprising to learn that Maria Caterina Lomellino's husband, Giuseppe Maria Garibaldi (one of the managers of the Teatro Falcone), took care of distributing the composer's possessions to his heirs, and not only kept Stradella's music for himself but tried later on to enlarge his personal collection of it, behaviour one would think too generous and full of respect for a nobleman towards a musician who had cuckolded him." This reservation is superficially appealing, but it is possible that Garibaldi's apparently "generous" conduct might have been well-calculated to protect his wife's virtue or to immunize his in-laws against criminal reputations.

One of the news bulletins from Genoa gave another reason for deadly anger of the Lomellino brothers against Stradella. According to this rumor, an actress had been impregnated and abandoned by a priest; Giovanni took the young woman under his protection but became jealous when he found that she was in love with Stradella.

It is difficult to choose between the two hypotheses that both point to guilt within the Lomellino family. However, despite the puzzles that remain about the details of the Stradella assassination plot, it is hard to escape the conclusion that the composer was undone by his old nemesis, revenge for love.

Bibliographical Notes

My source for the biography of Stradella is Carolyn Gianturco's *Alessandro Stradella, 1639–1682: His Life and Music* (Oxford: Clarendon Press, 1994), 262–65, 266–67, 33, 267–69, 272–73, 42, 56, 57, 59, 60. This includes, in Italian and English, Stradella's extant writings, among them twenty-four letters that have been translated into English and published for the first time. Gianturco opines that "many of the documents which [Remo] Giazotto cites" in his two-volume *Vita di Alessandro Stradella* (Milan: Curci, 1962) "cannot be found, whereas others which contradict them have since come to light." I note that Giazotto has misnamed Agnese Van Uffele, the first femme fatale in Stradella's life.

Ellen Rosand's review of Gianturco's biography appeared in the online *Journal of Seventeenth-Century Music* 1, 1 (1995), http://sscm-jscm.press.uiuc.edu/v1/no1/rosand.html (accessed Dec. 13, 2007).

The origin of the "Stradella myth" is in the biography of the composer in *Histoire de la musique depuis son origine, les progrès successifs de cet art jusqu' à présent, et la comparaison de la musique italienne et de la musique française* (Paris: C. Cochart, 1715), which was begun by Abbé Pierre Bourdelot, continued by Pierre Bonnet-Bourdelot, completed and published by Jacques Bonnet.

Friedrich Wilhelm Riese's libretto for Friedrich von Flotow's opera, *Alessandro Stradella,* is provided with the Capriccio two-CD recording 60117 of a 2004 production of Westdeutscher Rundfunk, Cologne, Germany.

Novelists have been attracted by Stradella's love affair with the Venetian nobleman's protégée. Examples include Marion Crawford, *Stradella* (New York: Macmillan, 1909); and Philippe Beaussant, *Stradella* (Paris: Gallimard, 1990). In Beaussant's novel the tradition that Stradella was spared assassination because of the beauty of his oratorio is found to be rooted in the myth of Orpheus, whose music charmed wild beasts. Beaussant comments, "A myth makes sense only if it is always true and if an Italian of the seventeenth century can repeat what already has been done. All I know is that the story of Stradella's music stirring the souls of the assassins to the point of disarming them has come down through the centuries. Everyone has believed it to be true, admirable and exemplary. Me too" (222).

6

The Tragic Night of Anton Webern

For many years an abundance of inconsistent theories were offered to account for the fatal shooting of composer Anton Webern on the evening of September 15, 1945, in Mittersill, an Alpine town southwest of Salzburg in the U.S.-occupied zone of Austria. It was a deadly response to a curfew violation, some said, when Webern stepped into the night air to enjoy an American cigar. Other explanations received by musicologist Hans Moldenhauer, who studied the riddle of Webern's sudden death, were more sinister: a well-known Swiss composer opined that the killing had been "intentional" and the result of a "criminal act," and the widow of a Viennese composer wrote to Moldenhauer of "rumors that [Webern's] Nazi son-in-law Benno Mattel had shot him."

In the last decade of his life, Anton Webern as a man and musician had been a victim of cultural totalitarianism and the Nazification of Europe. After leading a Mendelssohn program for Ravag (Radio Austria) in honor of the composer's birthday, he saw his career as a conductor come to an end. In the wake of the Anschluss, Webern's music was included in a Nazi propaganda exhibit of "Degenerate Art" in Vienna's Künstlerhaus. This official proscription made it impossible to have his works performed in his homeland or elsewhere in Nazi dominions. The income from his teaching also dwindled away.

Webern's biographers, including Hans Moldenhauer and Kathryn Bailey, have cited evidence that, despite the political oppression from which his career suffered, Webern was, during the first years of World War II, strangely attracted to Nazism. Kathryn Bailey writes that "in the early

1940s . . . Webern shows great enthusiasm for Hitler and Nazi domination as the German world's ordained and proper destiny." At least for a time Webern expressed admiration for Hitler as the force behind German resurgence. In a letter of March 4, 1940, to his friend Josef Hueber he wrote that a reading of *Mein Kampf* had brought him "much enlightenment." Bailey notes that, among Webern's children, only his daughter Maria Halbich managed "to resist the pull towards National Socialism." Perhaps in the interest of protecting his family, Webern maintained silence on the Nazi regime's anti-Semitism, a stance that upset Jewish friends and colleagues, notably Arnold Schoenberg and pianist Eduard Steuermann.

The last years of World War II brought tragedy and hardship to Webern and his family. In the spring of 1944 Webern, at age sixty, was inducted into service in the air raid protection police, living in a barrack away from his home in Mödling, a town outside Vienna. In March 1945 he learned of the death of his soldier son Peter, whose troop train was hit by low-flying Allied bombers. On March 31 Webern and his wife, Wilhelmine, their daughter Amalie, and her two children left Vienna on foot to join their other two daughters, Christine and Maria, and their families in Mittersill. The hope of the Weberns was to escape the bombings and privations of the Austrian capital.

For a while the entire Webern family lived together with Maria's in-laws, but Christine and her husband, Benno Mattel, moved to the rented ground floor of a house located "am Markt 101" on the outskirts of Mittersill. It was here that Anton and Wilhelmine were invited for dinner on the last evening of his life. After the meal was over, Webern was shot to death outside the front door.

In August 1959 Moldenhauer, accompanied by his wife, Rosaleen, made a pilgrimage to the site. In his 1961 book *The Death of Webern: A Drama in Documents,* Moldenhauer recalled that the marks left by the bullets that killed Webern were still visible: "I walked along the pathway up to the door. There, in the stucco wall next to the log frame, three bullet holes can still be seen. They are about waist high above the ground, two on the left, and one on the right side of the door. Three small holes puncturing the stone bespeak the violence which had struck here." The Moldenhauers spoke to the few Mittersill residents who remembered the shooting. They told the Moldenhauers that on the evening in question, American occupation soldiers were searching for Bruno Mattel, Webern's son-in-law, "who

Left: Anton Webern, 1945. Below: The house in Mittersill, Austria, where Webern was shot.

had made himself politically suspect." (Mattel was in fact a former storm trooper; he had married Christine Webern in his brown uniform.) While the Americans talked to Mattel in the kitchen, Webern left the house to smoke; since it was 10:00 he "apparently was mistaken for his son-in-law" and was shot at the moment he walked out of the house.

Moldenhauer's passion to discover the true circumstances of Webern's death impelled him to carry on painstaking inquiries of U.S. governmental and military offices and in November 1959 brought him a promising reply from the U.S. Army Records Center in St. Louis, Missouri. Records in that office showed that units of the 42nd (Rainbow) Division were located at Mittersill on the date of the shooting; the center's commanding officer furnished Moldenhauer the names and latest addresses of officers assigned to those units. This information, supplemented by a response of the Adjutant General's office, enabled Moldenhauer to write letters to two dozen men inquiring about their possible knowledge of facts concerning the shooting. One of the letters led Moldenhauer to a valuable source, Martin U. Heiman, who was attached to the 242nd Infantry Regiment of the Rainbow Division, which served in Mittersill in September 1945, and who acted as interpreter of German-speaking witnesses and investigator in the whole regimental area.

Heiman forwarded Moldenhauer a copy of his affidavit of December 28, 1959, recording his knowledge of circumstances of Webern's death. According to Heiman, on Saturday evening, September 15, 1945, he was called away from a dance to follow a man he knew well, a headquarters company cook, to "a nearby civilian home in order to help arrest a black marketeer, Benno Mattel, and to act as interpreter in a shooting which took place in this connection." The victim "lying dead from newly inflicted bullet wounds" on the ground floor opposite the kitchen was Anton von Webern. During the investigation Heiman acted as interpreter. The ensuing trial resulted in the imposition of a one-year jail sentence on Mattel for black market activities. The first sergeant and the cook who were involved in the arrest had contacted Mattel after learning that he "was a real or prospective black marketeer." With permission from superiors, the two soldiers took army food and supplies to Mattel's home on the evening of September 15 and negotiated sale prices. When Mattel agreed to the purchase, they drew their pistols and placed him under arrest. Heiman observed that the cook may not have been an ideal choice for a sting operation: "It should be noted at this time that the cook involved was even normally a very nervous person, easily aroused and excitable, even though—according to my knowledge—not a bad character and sometimes helpful."

The cook's high-strung nature may have played a key role in what transpired: "The cook—already in a very excited state—stepped out of the hallway and the house into the darkness and promptly bumped into a figure by whom he felt himself attacked. He fired 3 shots 'in self-defense' and kept on going to the restaurant to get the undersigned [Heiman]. . . . [Webern] only stepped outside the house shortly before, coming from the room across the hallway, to smoke an American cigar, given to him earlier by his son-in-law, B. Mattel." Additional details were provided in a statement of Wilhelmine Webern, a copy of which Heiman attached to his report. She confirmed that, at 9:45 P.M. exactly, her husband walked outside because "he wanted to smoke the cigar which he had received the same evening from our son-in-law." Webern "wanted to smoke it . . . outside the [bedroom] in order not to bother the children." Frau Webern discounted the cook's claim of self-defense: "My husband was reconvalescent and weighed only about 50 kilos (110 lbs.); he is about 160 cms (5'4") high. According to my belief it would be against his nature to attack anybody, especially a soldier."

In further correspondence Heiman was able to inform Moldenhauer that the last name of the cook who shot Webern was Bell. His report was accurate, because army records identified the cook as Raymond N. Bell. It turned out that Bell was deceased, but his wife, Helen, wrote graciously to Moldenhauer. Her husband had been a restaurant chef after the war and had died of alcoholism. She knew little about the accident except that it troubled her husband: "When he came home from the war he told me he killed a man in the line of duty. I knew he worried greatly over it. Everytime he became intoxicated, he would say, 'I wish I hadn't killed that man.' I truly think it helped to bring on his sickness. He was a very kind man who loved everyone. These are the results of war. So many suffer."

The persevering quest of Hans Moldenhauer did not put at rest the minds of commentators who have favored more sensational explanations of Webern's death. According to Kathryn Bailey, "most accounts have agreed that in stepping outside . . . Webern was breaking a curfew." The composer's 1966 biographer, Friedrich Wildgans, wrote that an 8:00 general curfew had recently been imposed but that, in view of the arrangements for the sting, Mattel had not been informed. This explanation justifiably does not satisfy Kathryn Bailey, who counters that "Wildgans fails to explain how it was that none of the (ten?) people living in the Halbich household [where Webern was living] knew about the curfew either." She regards as more plausible a speculation that "a special curfew had been placed on the house where the Mattels lived for this occasion only, and that the others living in the house had been told of the curfew but the Mattels naturally had not been, and that it had not occurred to anyone that the Mattels might have visitors that night."

The alternative supposition of a single-house curfew appears fanciful, particularly since such an order would have relied on the discretion of the Mattels' landlady, Elise Fritzenwanger, who, in the eyes of the American occupation authorities, would likely have been regarded as an enemy civilian. Rendering the special curfew thesis even more dubious is a further observation by Bailey. According to a written report by Mittersill's mayor, "the reason no one was allowed to leave the house was that it was being searched; no curfew is mentioned."

Other explanations of the Webern shooting are advanced by devotees of conspiracy theory. Conductor Hans Rosbaud suggested that Webern was clearly silhouetted in front of a lighted window and was therefore known to his killer. Disregarding the fact that Mattel was arrested, Louis Krasner retold a story that Webern had intentionally exposed himself to gunfire in order to allow his son-in-law to escape.

The random nature of the Mittersill shooting, which put a tragic end to the life and creativity of one of twentieth-century music's greatest geniuses, has inspired playwrights and opera composers to revisit the event. One of those to do so was poet-playwright James Schevill, who included "The Death of Anton Webern" in his *Collected Short Plays*. Schevill's "counterpoint for voices" on Webern's death, intended to be presented as a radio play, a concert reading, or a television piece with film or projections, was first performed by the Radio Players of San Francisco State University in 1967. Drawing on the factual revelations made by Moldenhauer, Schevill includes among his characters Webern, his wife, one of his daughters, his black-marketeer son-in-law, and the American cook who took the composer's life. The unifying plot element in the short drama is the ominous cigar. Webern's family recalls the composer's fondness for cigars. His daughter recalls that her "father composed through smoking cigars," and his widow muses affectionately,

Music and cigars . . . He smoked me out
Constantly from his study. I never really

Understood his music, so short, whispering angles,
Jumping rhythms, but I never heard it often.

Benno Mattel attributes the origin of the sting operation to his purchase
of the cigar that he gave to Webern:

At the door stood an American cook,
   A simple man, drawling a southern accent,
Who desired the pleasures of money.
   We drank as friends, even if it was I who joked.
   We celebrated war's end, the birth of leisure,
And he sold me the cigar to burn away my world.

And the ghost of Webern recalls how the pleasures of that cigar were ef-
faced by gunsmoke:

I stood in the doorway, savoring the smoke,
      the shape, the touch,
A sensuous man hoping for a return
        of the sensuous time,
Staring at the stars, the mountains
        huge over the quiet village . . .
I heard voices, turned back in alarm . . .
A frantic figure broke the darkness of the hall . . .
     I grappled with him . . .

The author attempts to imitate in Webern's mode of speech the jagged
rhythms and enigmatic silences of the composer's style. Webern's wife, Wilhelmine, reported in her statement to investigators that his last words were
"It's over." In Schevill's imaginative rendering, however, Webern prefers as
his finale the subtler markings in his scores, and he places the beauty and
inventiveness of his music above life's vicissitudes:

"It's over."
   The language of stupidity,
   of artificial life,
      not of music.

Like a whisper
  Scarcely audible
    Dying away
      The directions of my music,
Desires of intense, natural change,
        the constant changes of inconstancy,
the horror and beauty of opposed forces
            resolved by the ear,
        shifting structures
of mystery
              transcending death and time,
                crab-like movements,
                silent pauses . . .

British writer and film director Peter Greenaway has produced three versions of a surrealist work on murders of composers, including Anton Webern. Entitled at first *Rosa* and later given the additional name *The Death of a Composer,* Greenaway's enterprise successively took the form of a 1993 novel conceived as an elaborately annotated opera libretto without music; an opera, which premiered in 1994, with a libretto drawn from Greenaway's novel and music by Dutch composer Louis Andriessen; and a 1999 film adaptation for television. At the beginning of his novel, Greenaway describes the birth of his idea:

I have been interested for a long time in a melodramatic conspiracy against composers, and have talked and written about it in so many complicated ways, that I am no longer completely certain how to tell it any more. So anticipating credulity, I am going to write of it as though it was an opera, for perhaps opera is capable of indulging in concepts and illusions too preposterous to be tolerated in any form.

There are ten assassinations in the conspiracy. All of them are composers. At this stage you must believe that five of the composers are already dead. With dry ceremony their five coffins have been brought on to the stage. We are to consider the death of a sixth composer and to fill a sixth coffin. The composer's name is Rosa—Juan Manuel de Rosa, almost the same as the General, Juan Manuel de Rosas, who slaughtered two million South American Indians in Brazil in 1857.

Composer Rosa, like most in the sequence of ten victims conceived by Greenaway, is fictional; described as a writer of scores for Hollywood Westerns who was fonder of his black horse Ebola than of his fiancée Esmeralda, he was found dead in an abandoned slaughterhouse in Fray Bentos, Uruguay, in 1956. But the first and last in Greenaway's series of murdered composers were tragically real, Anton Webern and John Lennon.

A passage in the novel *Rosa* invokes the mysteries associated in history and myth with the sudden deaths of composers: "The death of a composer needs investigating. Was Mozart poisoned? Was Tchaikovsky murdered? Was Webern assassinated? Was Orpheus really slaughtered? Was Rosa murdered in mysterious circumstances in Fray Bentos? He was shot by mysterious assailants whilst riding his horse. Who were the murderers?" Broom-sweepers who clean the blood of the abattoir ask, "Who would ever want to kill a composer?" and the novel's text replies only with more questions: "Is it indeed a fact that Rosa was killed because he was a composer? It might have been because Rosa was a fornicator and an abuser of women. Or an abuser of horses? Or was it because he abused his talent writing trash for the movies? Who says it was trash?"

Toward the novel's end, Greenaway introduces the Investigatrix to identify the principal pieces of evidence in Rosa's murder. In an apparent send-up of assassination conspiracy theories, the Investigatrix promises that

> we can show you that the death was not
> Coincidental
> And no random assassination.
> There are clues that unite this death of a famous
> composer to a conspiracy.

Winnowing her findings, the Investigatrix finds ten clues present at the death of each of the ten composers linked together in a series of murders— "a hat, a pair of spectacles, a smoking cigar, a gun, three bullets, vegetation, night, a grieving widow, American passports and a composer." Most of these circumstances are so frequently present at the scenes of composers' deaths, regardless of their cause, that they do not go far to sustain the Investigatrix's claim to have discovered an overarching criminal design. But buried in this joke at the would-be sleuth's expense, a juxtaposition of certain clues points suggestively to Anton Webern's death. Is he not the only historical composer in Greenaway's series who, while smoking a cigar, was shot in the night with three bullets by a killer of American nationality and who left behind a grieving widow?

In "Filming Opera," an "open discussion" held in August 2000 with the European Graduate School on the filming of *Rosa*, Greenaway revealed that since the 1970s he had been "deeply fascinated" by the death of Anton Webern, saying, "There are lots of theories about his death because nobody could actually believe that it was so peculiarly accidental." Greenaway's acquaintance with the facts of the case seems sketchy. He remarks that "three shots suddenly rang out and the man lay dying in the snow. He was dead twenty-four hours afterward." But Greenaway's wildest contribution to the catalog of myths about Webern's shooting is his reference to a theory that the composer, born into a Roman Catholic family ennobled in the sixteenth century, "recently had converted from Judaism to Christianity and this was a reprisal by some very keen Zionists." Greenaway also referred to suggestions that "departing Nazis had a particular antagonism to anybody who subverted the German tradition of music" and that Webern was "embroiled in some dubious associations with his son-in-law." The filmmaker added mysteriously that "there were also some extenuating [*sic*] circumstances surrounding his autopsy." This accumulation of "fiction" and "apocrypha" led to the director's decision to "make something fictional" of Webern's death. In the discussion of the televising of *Rosa*, Greenaway (perhaps with his tongue firmly planted in his cheek) purported to have discovered a link between Webern's death and the 1980 murder of John Lennon. He "noticed that there were a remarkable number of clues present at the death of John Lennon, exactly the same clues present so much earlier at the death of Anton Webern."

Christopher Bernard, a writer of poetry, fiction, plays, and journalism and the founder of an online literary and arts magazine, *Caveat Lector,* is the composer and librettist of an opera, "Nachtstück: An Opera on the Death of Anton Webern," which was given a reading at the Playwrights' Center of San Francisco on August 14, 1992. The opera's action begins with the entry of Webern, the only named character, into his son-in-law's garden after the family dinner of September 15, 1945. A military loudspeaker announces a curfew beginning at exactly 9:30 P.M., and a fresh poster near the garden gate warns that violators may be shot. "Our new occupiers!" Webern muses. "But better than the others." He lights his cigar, three gunshots sound, and he reels as if struck. The light on Webern fades.

When the mountains brighten, the play takes a retrospective turn. Webern reappears overcome with guilt, regretting his belief in Hitler and his betrayal of his friendship with Arnold Schoenberg. Images of trains carrying Jews to death camps haunt him, and he laments his failure to save his son Peter's life by leaving before the war. A fantasy of his own death in a curfew violation appeases a sense of justice:

> There is a gate that leads outside here.
> If I leave by it,
> I'll meet a patrol
> of the Americans
> and be shot, no questions asked.
> The Germans were no kinder!
> It would be "poetic justice":
> maybe my folly deserves no better.
> Such a death will be forgotten quickly,
> a minor incident of the occupation—
> regrettable, to be sure, but to be expected:
> at any rate, the victim should not have been
> taking his constitutional after curfew. . . .
> It would be a fair punishment.

These reflections introduce what Bernard terms an "opera within an opera," based on the historical Webern's unpublished 1913 play in six scenes, "Tod" (Death), inspired by the death of a nephew. Webern observes a Man and Woman in grief over their lost child and draws a parallel to his own suffering over the death of Peter:

> My nephew
> died that summer
> just before
> the other war—
> I wrote my dream out,
> then forgot it,
> It comes again.

The earlier family tragedy is resolved when the Woman is confronted by the dead child's guardian angel and the Man recognizes that "our life on earth is the image of eternity." The Man sees the hand of God in the beauty of the mountains:

> A mountain flower shows that beauty,
> uncanny in its perfection,
> the tenderness,
> the holiness
> of the nameless One.

The light on the forestage goes up, showing Webern once more at the garden gate. He expresses hope that he will "build a life of good" in his music and will have "just enough time to erase that memory that hounds" him. But the three gunshots are heard again and Webern intones the last three words that he spoke in life: "It is over."

In May 1998 a ludicrous hoax linking Anton Webern's music to the Nazi SS circulated on the Internet. An article originally attributed to an author bearing the transnational name "Heinrich Kincaid" and supposedly copyrighted by the Associated Press headlined its revelations: "Composer Webern Was Double Agent for Nazis." A sampling of Kincaid's disclosures makes his attempt at heavy-handed satire apparent:

> BERLIN, GERMANY (AP)—Recent admissions by an ex-Nazi official living in Argentina have confirmed what some musicologists have suspected for years: that early twentieth century German composer Anton Webern and his colleagues devised the so-called "serial" technique of music to encrypt messages to Nazi spies living in the United States and Britain.
>
> In what can surely be considered the most brazen instance of Art Imitating Espionage to date, avant garde composers of the Hitler years working in conjunction with designers of the Nazi Enigma code were bamboozling unsuspecting audiences with their atonal thunderings while at the same time passing critical scientific data back and forth between nations. . . .
>
> It is now known that Webern was using music to shuttle Werner Heisenberg's discoveries in atomic energy to German spy Klaus Fuchs working on the Manhattan atom bomb project in New Mexico. Due to the secret nature of the project, which was still underway

after the invasion of Berlin, Army officials at the time were unable to describe the true reason for Webern's murder.

Hans Scherbius, a Nazi party official who worked with Minister of Propaganda Joseph Goebbels, admitted at age eighty-seven that the Nazis secretly were behind the twelve-tone technique of composition, which was officially reviled to give it the outlaw status it needed to remain outside of the larger public purview.

"These pieces were nothing more than cipher for encoding messages," he chuckled during an interview on his balcony in Buenos Aires. "It was only because it was 'naughty' and difficult that elite audiences accepted it, even championed it."

Arnold Schonberg [*sic*], the older musician who first devised the serial technique at the request of the Weimar government of Germany, composed in America to deliver bomb data stolen by Fuchs back to the Nazis, who worked feverishly to design their own atomic weapons.

As an example, Scherbius showed Associated Press reporters the score of Webern's Opus 30 "Variations for Orchestra" overlaid with a cardboard template. The notes formed a mathematical grid that deciphered into German a comparison between the neutron release cross-sections of uranium isotopes 235 and 238.

Schonberg responded with a collection of songs for soprano and woodwinds that encrypted the chemical makeup of the polonium-beryllium initiator at the core of the Trinity explosion.

Exposure of the Webern hoax was soon to follow. Under a dateline of June 29, 1998, "Urban Legends and Folklore," an online series on About. com, published a "short list of factual errors and logical inconsistencies" in Kincaid's article, "more than sufficient to debunk the central claims." Included in the errors were the following howlers:

1. Klaus Fuchs spied for Russia, not Germany.
2. Why would "Arnold Schoenberg, a Jew who fled Nazi oppression in Germany in 1933, spy for the Third Reich"?
3. The author of About.com's rebuttal could "find no evidence that a 'Hans Scherbius,' the supposed 'Nazi party official' who was the source of these shocking revelations, actually existed."

On July 3, 1998, American composer Chris Hertzog supplemented this list with the observation that Arnold Schoenberg's famous article explaining his invention of twelve-tone serial composition appeared in the 1920s, long before the Nazis came to power.

Although the Webern Internet hoax was readily detected, the surviving riddle is why its originator found amusement in suggesting a tie between the composer and the Nazi cause. It is possible that the deviser of the scheme was aware of Webern's temporary enthusiasms over the Nazi conquest of Europe. However, this is a relatively obscure chapter in the composer's life that would not resonate in the minds of many blog readers. It is also apparent that Webern is by no means the sole butt of Kincaid's espionage joke; he also included Arnold Schoenberg, an eminent Jewish refugee from Nazi persecution, among the agents in his fictitious spy network. Therefore, Nazi sympathies can be put aside as the satirist's principal target. More likely, the Internet jest is at the expense of twelve-tone music, which, Kincaid suggests, could not have been invented to please the ear and must therefore have been meant to transmit covert messages.

Bibliographical Notes

The principal source concerning the death of Anton Webern remains Hans Moldenhauer, *The Death of Anton Webern: A Drama in Documents* (New York: Philosophical Library, 1961). The facts revealed in this work are reaffirmed in Hans Moldenhauer, in collaboration with Rosaleen Moldenhauer, *Anton von Webern: A Chronicle of His Life and Work* (New York: Knopf, 1979). I also consulted Friedrich Wildgans, *Anton Webern* (New York: October House, 1967); Malcolm Hayes, *Anton von Webern* (London: Phaidon, 1995); and Kathryn Bailey, *The Life of Webern* (Cambridge, England: Cambridge Univ. Press, 1998), 164–91.

James Schevill's play *The Death of Anton Webern* is included in his *Collected Short Plays* (Athens: Swallow Press/Ohio Univ. Press, 1986), 235–44. The novel that begins the *Rosa* project is Peter Greenaway, *Rosa* (Paris: Editions Dis Voir, 1993), 48, 84, 106–14. Peter Greenaway's discussion with the European Graduate School in August 2000, "Filming Opera," is found at http://www.egs.edu/faculty/greenaway/greenaway-opera-2000.html (accessed Oct. 6, 2007). Author Christopher Bernard kindly provided me a copy of the unpublished libretto of "Nachtstück: An Opera on the Death of Anton Webern," 7, 13, 22, 29, 39, 44.

For text and commentary relating to the Webern Internet hoax, see About.com: Urban Legends and Folklore, "Webern's Dodecaphonic Conspiracy," June 29, 1998, http://urbanlegends.about.com/library/weekly/aa062998.htm (accessed Oct. 6, 2007); "More on the Webern—Nazi Hoax," About.com: Urban Legends and Folklore, July 3, 1998, http://urbanlegends.about.com/library/weekly/aa070398.htm (accessed Oct. 7, 2007).

7

The Deadly Vacation of Marc Blitzstein

Whenever Marc Blitzstein undertook stage works on themes of crime and punishment, trouble lay ahead. His first attempt was a two-act ballet, *Cain* (1930), in which the world's first murderer is slain by Lamech, one of his descendants. Lamech is cursed by Jehovah and receives the mark of Cain as onlookers bury their faces in fear. Jehovah raises His voice again and curses the entire people; as they lift their heads, all their brows are seen to bear the mark of Cain. In the introduction to the scenario, Blitzstein moralizes, "Thus murder, begun in our world by Cain, is perpetuated through the ages: we are all the sons of Cain." To his great disappointment, the score was rejected by Leopold Stokowski and remained unperformed until 2008, when it was included in the American Composers Alliance's "Festival of American Music."

Blitzstein's second musical setting of a crime subject was *The Condemned* (1932), a short choral opera inspired by two of his labor heroes, Sacco and Vanzetti, who are embodied in the title character, sung in four-part male voices; the remaining roles are taken by the Wife, the Friend, and the Priest, each performed in multiple voices. The three comforters attempt to bring solace on the day of execution, but the Condemned's own inner strength enables him to face his death with equanimity: "I need no heaven. The earth shall one day be enough. All men are my brothers." Although *The Condemned* was never produced, it led by indirection to Blitzstein's conception of a larger work, a full-scale opera presenting the trial and execution of Sacco and Vanzetti. Blitzstein's biographer, Eric A. Gordon, relates that during the composer's visit to Rome in 1959, Italian music critic

Fedele D'Amico, having remembered *The Condemned,* gave him an anarchist pamphlet describing Sacco and Vanzetti as "two victims of American-Dollar Justice." The tract moved Blitzstein to study the history of the case, and he concluded that it had the makings of an opera. It was while he was still considering alternative means of treatment that the Ford Foundation announced its grant of $950,000 to four opera companies, including the Metropolitan Opera, for the production of new American works. Blitzstein obtained a Ford Foundation grant of $15,000, payable over two years, for his proposed opera, *Sacco and Vanzetti,* optioned for production by the Metropolitan.

Cries of outrage were heard from conservative journalists when the historical theme of the commissioned work became known. One of the strongest invectives was hurled by George Sokolsky, who made apparent reference to Blitzstein's 1958 testimony in an executive session of the House Committee on Un-American Activities that he had been a member of the Communist Party between 1938 and 1949. The columnist could not understand how the Metropolitan Opera had agreed to stage an opera "about a pair of anarchists . . . written by one who at a telling period in the history of his country was a Communist which means that he had submitted to the discipline of the Kremlin—a government which since 1917 was an enemy of his country."

Fully predictable, these expressions of right-wing anger were a minor irritant; Blitzstein's problems with *Sacco and Vanzetti* were artistic rather than political. Perhaps it was simply too late in his career for him to shoulder a major operatic assignment on his own. The undertaking of a vast musical drama was particularly daunting because Blitzstein insisted on writing his own libretto, a task that he had recently performed with difficulty. In a 1951 letter to his close friend Mina Curtiss, written while working on his Broadway opera *Reuben Reuben,* he lamented, "Why the hell can't I have a collaborator at this point?" The opera took Blitzstein six years to complete and closed during a Boston tryout in 1955. Now, the subject that Blitzstein was to dramatize and score was the most formidable he had ever chosen; the complexity of the Sacco and Vanzetti life histories and of the related trials would require extensive study and pruning of source material by Blitzstein before he could make substantial headway in penning words or music.

It is small wonder that the two-year grant period expired without delivery of Blitzstein's work product to the Metropolitan, and in November

1960 the Ford Foundation declined his request for an additional payment of $7,500. In many ways, Blitzstein began to exhibit symptoms of writer's block. Even casual inquiries about his progress enraged him, as he diverted his attention from the opera project by filling his calendar with vacations, travel, minor compositions, and an engagement to teach playwriting (hardly his strong suit) at Bennington College during the 1962–63 academic year.

In November 1963 he traveled to Martinique, where he planned to spend the winter in a villa near the town of Frégate-François on the island's Atlantic coast. He left his drafts of *Sacco and Vanzetti* behind, telling a friend, composer David Diamond, that he intended to work instead on his score for a one-act opera based on Bernard Malamud's story "Idiots First." He did not live to complete either of these works; the public learned in a shocking Associated Press news report of January 24, 1964, that Blitzstein was "killed in an auto accident Wednesday night [January 22] on the West Indian island of Martinique" where he had been "working on several new operas, including one based on the Sacco-Vanzetti case."

This version of Blitzstein's death lasted only one day. On January 25, the *New York Times* published a police announcement of "the arrest of three sailors on charges of having fatally beaten the American composer Marc Blitzstein." The police said that "two Portuguese sailors and one from Martinique, whose names were not released, got into a dispute with the composer Tuesday night and beat him." The details, according to the *New York Times,* were "sketchy." The police had "taken the composer to a hospital, where he died, after treatment, 24 hours later." The three suspects had been "drunk at the time of the attack on the composer."

An attorney for the Blitzstein family had told the *New York Times* about information given a family member by twenty-eight-year-old William Milam, U.S. vice consul in Martinique, that the police were investigating "something suspicious about the death." The *Philadelphia Bulletin* also quoted Milam as saying that "the facts show it was a robbery." The U.S. consular report of February 3, 1964, linked the attack on Blitzstein to his composition of *Sacco and Vanzetti,* stating that "the victim was visiting those dives [where he encountered the sailors] to find color for the opera he was writing here."

From the hints dropped in these sources, Blitzstein's friends in America formed their own speculations about the circumstances of the Martinique assault. Composer Virgil Thomson opined that the "dispute" between the composer and his assailants was a quarrel about politics. The alternative theory that Blitzstein had visited the wrong part of town in search of local color could have rung true to some who were familiar with the intended plot of *Sacco and Vanzetti:* one of the characters was to be a Portuguese murder convict, Celestino Madeiros.

The brief accounts of the attackers' sentencing added little information to the public's understanding of the crime. On April 1, 1965, the *New York Times* reported: "Two Portuguese sailors and a Martinique youth were convicted today of assault and theft in connection with the death of the American composer Marc Blitzstein. The Portugese sentences of 14 months [Alfred Mendez Rodriguez, age thirty-four] and three years [Armando Fernandez, age twenty-six] respectively." The "Martinique youth," Daniel Yves Charles Nicolas, only seventeen, after a trial held in secret because of his minority status, received a fourteen-month suspended sentence and three years' probation. The reason that none of the sailors was charged with homicide was evidently the absence of an intent to kill.

More precise details of the verdict rendered by three judges and nine jurors are contained in a judgment entered March 31, 1965, by the trial court (Cour d'Assises) of Martinique. The text identifies Armando Fernandez as the principal criminal, who, in violation of provisions of the French Penal Code (deriving from the Napoleonic Penal Code of 1810), "intentionally" beat and wounded Blitzstein in circumstances where the blows and injuries were "inflicted without the intent to cause death but nevertheless resulted in it." The other two defendants were convicted of having "in the same circumstances of time and place" stolen from Blitzstein "the sum of ninety francs, a half dollar, a pair of pants, car keys and a wristwatch," under circumstances justifying the application of penal laws to the teenage defendant. According to the verdict, the crimes committed by the three sailors involved elements of both aggravation and mitigation. Blitzstein's unintended death increased the maximum penalty for Fernandez's attack to imprisonment for a term of ten to twenty years; the robbery entailed an enhanced maximum prison sentence of five to ten years because the crime was perpetrated at night by two or more persons. All the penalties actually imposed, however, were far below these authorized ranges, since the court and the jury found that the defendants were entitled to the benefit of "extenuating circumstances." As was typical in French verdicts of the era, the nature of extenuating circumstances that were weighed in favor of Blitzstein's attackers is left unstated. The juvenile defendant escaped his legal ordeal with only a suspended prison sentence and a term of probation to admonish lightly his role in Blitzstein's death; his mother was ordered to pay a civil fine to reimburse the cost of his condemnation. The Guadeloupe-Martinique newspaper, *France-Antilles,* in an article of April 2, 1965, justified the generous treatment of the minor by evidence that his participation in the crimes was "minimal."

Lillian Hellman, whose play *The Little Foxes* received an operatic setting in Blitzstein's *Regina* (1949), was dissatisfied with the outcome of the investigation and trial; she decided to explore the case anew. In his 1989 biography *Mark the Music: The Life and Work of Marc Blitzstein,* Eric Gordon summarizes the fruitless result of Hellman's mission to Martinique aboard Hollywood producer Sam Spiegel's luxurious yacht: "She told [the consul] how she felt that Marc had not been properly cared for. William Milam and James DeCou [the U.S. Public Information Officer] understood her grief but patiently laid out the facts of the case. It was a confirmation of her worst fears. She invited the consul to lunch on the yacht, and that was the investigation." In the biography, Gordon undertakes a detailed reconstruction of the assault on the composer. The sources of his account apparently included interviews or communications with Milam and DeCou, with whom Hellman had spoken, but there is no indication that he had access to any judicial findings.

Gordon relates that on the night of January 21, 1964, after dining with George and Lollie Peckham, new friends he had made in Martinique, Blitzstein did not return to his villa nearby. Instead, he drove across the island into Fort-de-France. The biographer states that the purpose of Blitzstein's nocturnal visit was "to check out the scene down at the waterfront bars where the sailors and merchant seamen liked to drink. Shortly before midnight, he fell in with three such types, two Portuguese and a native Martiniquan, and together they toured several of the low-class dives around the Place de Stalingrad."

Disaster followed. "As they drank, Blitzstein fished for bills from his wallet, revealing the tidy sum he was carrying. After two or three hours, en route to the next bar, Blitzstein and one of his three companions slipped into a nearby alleyway, the lure of sex in the air. The other two followed. Then suddenly, all three set upon him. They beat him severely, robbed him of his valuables, and left him there in the alley stripped of every piece of clothing but his shirt and socks. Hearing his cries and moans, policemen found him between three and four in the morning and took him to Clarac Hospital." At the hospital Blitzstein at first told the staff that he had been injured in a car accident but later confided to Vice Consul Milam that he had been "robbed and beaten by three Venezuelans, which is what he believed his companions were." According to Gordon's account, Blitzstein also "admitted to some sexual advances with the men," but asked that this statement be kept confidential. Acting at Blitzstein's request, the consulate telegraphed his sister that he was hospitalized in an auto accident; she was further advised that her presence was needed. In the evening of January 22, Blitzstein died of his injuries. Gordon reflects, "What to three sailors seemed like a merry, drunken episode of beating up a queer and humiliating him by leaving him naked and stealing his money turned fatal under less than ideal hospital conditions to a man with a weak liver and in need of a hernia operation."

Martinique police found about $400 of Blitzstein's money in a cabin on the vessel of the three arrested sailors. Gordon notes that, in his conversation with American officials, "Police Chief Georges Fluchaire . . . spoke in confidential tones of his knowledge of Blitzstein as . . . a man of strange morals."

The view of Eric Gordon that Blitzstein's death resulted from a misadventure in the search for "rough trade" sex accords with entries in the memoirs of his friend, American composer Ned Rorem. Marc Blitzstein, Rorem noted, "forever championed the working class but avoided rubbing elbows with them unless they were rough trade . . . he was murdered by rough trade on the isle of Martinique by three seafarers of the very type he had spent a lifetime defending." However, not everyone in the creative arts community is persuaded that the circumstances of Blitzstein's death are established beyond doubt. Film director and actor Tim Robbins, in his book on the filming of *Cradle Will Rock,* leaves open the issue of the assailants' motivation: "Whether his murder was a result of gay bashing, a robbery gone awry, or a combination of both is impossible to know for sure."

When William Milam spoke to me in a telephone interview in February 2008, his memories of Blitzstein's death were remarkably bright. Over the course of his distinguished career in the U.S. Foreign Service, Milam rose from his position as junior consular officer in Martinique to ambassadorships in Bangladesh and Pakistan. In 2003 he became a Woodrow Wilson Center Senior Policy Scholar in Washington, D.C. Milam recalls that when Blitzstein arrived in Martinique, he registered at the consulate. Milam was aware that the newcomer was a composer, but only in the wake of the later tragedy did he come to understand Blitzstein's eminence in the American music world. Since Blitzstein was wintering in Frégate-François, Milam met him only occasionally after his registration. The two men crossed paths from time to time at the U.S. Information Services Library.

By an odd coincidence, their last encounter was early in the evening on the fateful date of January 21, 1964. After leaving the consulate at the end of the day's work, Milam found that he could not immediately drive home because his parked car was blocked in by other cars. To while away time until the obstruction cleared, he headed for a bar in a nearby hotel. Blitzstein, seated at a barroom table with two male companions (neither of them, Milam reflected later, could have been among the attackers), waved to Milam, inviting him to join them. Milam did so, and as the conversation proceeded in French, the vice consul had a comforting thought: he had never prided himself on his command of French, but Blitzstein clearly was laboring under greater difficulties with the language.

In the following midday, Milam received a call from a staff member of Clarac Hospital, who asked him to visit an American citizen who was under their care following a car accident. When Milam arrived at the hospital, he found Blitzstein lying on a gurney in a hallway. Milam had previously been given to understand that the injured man had either been involved in a collision or had been hit by a car while walking. At some point, however, Blitzstein gestured to him to come close and whispered that he had been attacked. Milam does not recall Blitzstein confessing to having made sexual advances. It was only later that the vice consul received a more detailed account of the attack from his friend, police chief Fluchaire, and it may be that Blitzstein made his admission to him. The police chief told Milam that the sailors were after Blitzstein's money, plain and simple; he had been "throwing his money around in the bars." The sailors pulled him outside in pursuit of his cash; the victim had chosen a "rough area" for his bar-hopping.

During his hospital visit, Milam pondered over Blitzstein's urgent need for medical attention, and his mind shot back to his barroom conversation of the day before when Blitzstein had shown his woeful limitations in French. The vice consul firmly believed that the patient must have an English-speaking physician taking part in his care; he arranged for a doctor of mixed American and French parentage to be present at the examination. The medical intervention was, however, unable to save Blitzstein's life.

Milam learned the cause of death from a Martinique investigative magistrate, whom he knew socially. The magistrate attributed the death to *éclatement de foie* (bursting of the liver). From this pronouncement,

Milam deduced that the three sailors not only beat Blitzstein savagely but probably kicked him as he lay on the ground.

Answering a question that nags at my mind, Milam is inclined to agree with the hypothesis, expounded in Eric Gordon's biography, that the sailors stripped Blitzstein to stigmatize him as a homosexual. Another puzzle of the case still eludes him: it is not clear how the police were able to identify and arrest the assailants. Milam doubts that Blitzstein could have been of much help to the investigation. (It should be noted, though, that in the hospital the mortally injured man had been close to correct in referring to the Portuguese as "Venezuelans"; they had taken Venezuelan citizenship.) Milam speculates that police work may have been aided by the fact that there were usually few vessels in Fort-de-France's harbor.

When the sailors' cases came up for trial, Milam's friend, the investigative magistrate, called him to request his testimony. But Milam's superior, Consul Arva Floyd, did not want him to testify, since he, like information officer James DeCou, wanted as little publicity as possible for an act of violence in the Caribbean paradise. The Blitzstein family was represented by a Martiniquan lawyer during courtroom proceedings.

Fifteen years after the assault on Blitzstein, the facts of his death, never disclosed with precision by Martinique authorities, left only hazy imprints on the islanders' memories. In 1979 the *New Yorker* included in its series "Our Far-Flung Correspondents" Truman Capote's account of his visit to an aristocratic Martinique woman living in Fort-de-France. Capote's short piece "Music for Chameleons," later the title story of a like-named collection, is haunted by references to the killing of Blitzstein. Observing that her guest seems to be a traveler, the elderly hostess inquires why he has not visited Martinique before. Unknowingly, she has turned their conversation toward Blitzstein, a subject that will be uncomfortable for them both:

> "Martinique? Well, I felt a certain reluctance. A good friend was murdered here."
>
> Madame's lovely eyes are a fraction less friendly than before. She makes a slow pronouncement: "Murder is a rare occurrence here. We are not a violent people. Serious, but not violent."

"Madame" steers their talk in safer directions, but she cannot avoid returning to the murder.

"And so you had a friend who was murdered here?"

"Yes."

"An American?"

"Yes. He was a very gifted man. A musician. A composer."

"Oh, I remember—the man who wrote operas! Jewish. He had a mustache."

"His name was Marc Blitzstein."

Before the story ends, Capote's hostess compulsively probes her further recollections of the American composer. He was a dinner guest when her husband was alive, played the piano and sang German songs. She asks Capote to remind her of the circumstances of the killing but balks when he calls it "an appalling tragedy." It was "a tragic accident," she insists and adds, "But our police caught those sailors. They were tried and sentenced and sent to prison in Guiana. . . . Those wretches ought to have been guillotined." The author of *In Cold Blood* could not have been expected to agree, but he replied that he "wouldn't mind seeing them at work in the fields in Haiti, picking bugs off coffee plants."

For several anxious months in 1964, it was thought that the work-in-progress for *Sacco and Vanzetti* was lost. When Leonard Bernstein announced at a memorial concert for Blitzstein on April 19 that the opera manuscript had apparently disappeared, the audience, according to Eric Gordon, "reacted in audible shock." On May 12, however, Theodore Strongin reported in the *New York Times* that the manuscript of the partly completed work "had been found in some cartons in the trunk of Mr. Blitzstein's automobile, after it was put up for sale after his death." A news release of the Metropolitan Opera added details: "The manager of the used car lot had noted some cartons in the trunk. When he read a statement from Mr. Bernstein in the newspapers referring to the missing manuscript he checked the cartons and found the partly completed opera." Leonard Bernstein was quoted as saying that "the first and second acts seemed to be substantially finished and that the third act had been sketched." He also commented that "the vast amount of material would have to be carefully studied before its final content could be determined." A cautionary note, however, was sounded by the Metropolitan: the only part of the work the company had seen was an aria for Sacco, "With a Woman to Be."

Eventually Bernstein declined to attempt completion of *Sacco and*

Vanzetti; he also abandoned his attempt to finish *Idiots First,* on which Blitzstein had been working in Martinique.

American composer Leonard J. Lehrman, an admirer of Blitzstein's work, came to the rescue. He completed *Idiots First* in 1973; the opera was produced with a two-piano accompaniment by the Bel Canto Opera in New York and won the 1978 Off-Broadway Opera award as the "most important event of the season." In 1992 the work received its orchestral premiere by the Center for Contemporary Opera at New York University.

Lehrman's task of fashioning *Sacco and Vanzetti* into a performable opera was much more demanding. He told a symposium on December 1, 1995, of the fragmentary state in which he found Blitzstein's manuscript. "Blitzstein told the Met [October 9, 1961] that as per the contract that he had, he had completed 75% of the libretto and 40% of the music. That was an exaggeration. You can see the music over there, and in sheer bulk there probably is about 40% of the music. But it contains multiple drafts of many, many scenes. I would say that he had completed 40% of parts of the music and 75% of the libretto." Blitzstein completed only one scene, Act One, Scene 3, in which Sacco and Vanzetti are arrested; he had not undertaken any sketches of orchestration.

On August 17–19, 2001, *Sacco and Vanzetti* received its first complete performances, with piano, at the White Barn in Westport, Connecticut. The ill fortune that afflicted the opera since its conception continued to make its presence known. Although many reviewers praised the work, Joel Honig, in an article for *Opera News,* scathingly attacked Lehrman's score as unfaithful to Blitzstein even though Honig had not attended a performance. The intemperate critic did not even spare Blitzstein from attack, charging that he had intentionally destroyed his last major work by suicidally inducing the sailors' attack on the Martinique waterfront: "Early in 1964, while vacationing in Martinique, Blitzstein was robbed and savagely beaten to death by three sailors in an alley outside a waterfront dive. In retrospect, it seems almost suicidal that the normally circumspect composer should have taken such a risk. He could not have been overly preoccupied with Sacco and Vanzetti, or concerned that such a heavy-duty pickup could go fatally awry." It remains to be seen whether full-scale performances of *Sacco and Vanzetti* may someday cause the opera to triumph over Blitzstein's violent death and to take its place among his memorable theater works, including *The Cradle Will Rock, Regina,* and the translation of the book and lyrics for the longest-running production of *The Threepenny Opera.*

Bibliographical Notes

The principal biographical and bibliographical sources on Marc Blitzstein are Eric A. Gordon, *Mark the Music: The Life and Work of Marc Blitzstein* (New York: St. Martin's, 1989); and Leonard J. Lehrman, *Marc Blitzstein: A Bio-Bibliography* (Westport, Conn.: Praeger, 2005). I have also cited reports of the Associated Press and the *New York Times* regarding the death of Blitzstein and the discovery of the *Sacco and Vanzetti* manuscript materials.

The following works of Marc Blitzstein are referred to in this chapter: *Cain* (a ballet, 1930), *The Condemned* (1932), *The Cradle Will Rock* (1936), *Regina* (1946–49), *Reuben Reuben* (1949–55), *Juno* (1957–59), *Sacco and Vanzetti* (1959–64, completed by Leonard J. Lehrman), *Idiots First* (1962–67, completed by Leonard J. Lehrman).

A copy of the judgment against Blitzstein's assailants was provided to me with a letter in the names of the prosecutor and the presiding judge of the Court of Appeals of Fort-de-France.

Ned Rorem comments on Blitzstein's death in his memoir *Knowing When to Stop* (New York: Simon and Schuster, 1994), 104, 313. Tim Robbins's speculations on alternative theories concerning Blitzstein's death are quoted from his book, *Cradle Will Rock: The Movie and the Moment* (New York: Newmarket Press, 2000), 61.

Truman Capote's Martinique travel piece, "Music for Chameleons," appears in *Music for Chameleons* (New York: Random House, 1980), 3–12.

Symposia held in 1995 and 2001 on Leonard Lehrman's completion of Blitzstein's *Sacco and Vanzetti* are found respectively at *Opera Journal* 29, 1 (1996): 26–46; and http://www.artists-in-residence.com/ljlehrman/articles/operajournal 8.html (accessed Oct. 5, 2007). Joel Honig's harsh criticism of the work (which he had not seen performed) was published as "Dead Man Writing," *Opera News* 66, 5 (2001): 88.

John Caldwell Ellis's play, *Blitzstein Strikes Back,* with songs by Blitzstein, has been given readings by the Neighborhood Playhouse and the American Renaissance Theater Company in New York City. The three sailors who attacked Blitzstein recurrently appear as wordless intruders into the play's action.

8

The Stalking of John Lennon

In his rapidly cycling moods, Mark David Chapman, born in 1955, experienced feelings of worthlessness and grandiosity. To Jack Jones, who interviewed him for more than 200 hours at Attica prison, he said in explanation of his murder of John Lennon: "I was an acute nobody. I had to usurp someone else's importance, someone else's success. I was 'Mr. Nobody' until I killed the biggest Somebody on earth." Before the murder, however, he liked to tell his wife, Gloria, that "ever since he was a kid he knew he was meant for greatness, that he was destined to be someone big." He was encouraged in this belief by his mother, who often fled to her young son's bedroom to escape marital violence.

On a morning after his sleep was disturbed by sounds of a quarrel in his parents' bedroom, Mark was visited by an apparition of the "Little People," who seemed to inhabit the walls of his bedroom and acclaimed him as their king. He could not remember when they had first come to him, but they were to return at emotional junctures of his life. The Little People witnessed a childhood and a coming-of-age that passed through many phases typical of the 1960s generation. After suffering indignities at the hands of schoolyard bullies, Mark began to experiment with psychedelic drugs, a curiosity the Beatles' *Magical Mystery Tour* album had first piqued. In 1970 he ran away from his suburban Atlanta home in the hope of finding a sense of belonging among the drug "freaks" of Miami. His job as a carnival security guard and his hippie acquaintanceship proved equally disappointing, and within months the prodigal returned to his dependent mother and unaffectionate father.

By 1971 Mark Chapman had remade himself once more, giving up drugs for born-again Christianity. Michael McFarland, a new friend who invited him to play guitar in a Christian rock band, recommended that he read *The Catcher in the Rye*. When Mark finished the novel, he was swept by a new conversion—to the personality of the book's hero, Holden Caulfield, and his campaign against phoniness. A childhood friend observed that Chapman had undergone a "true personality split," resolving to be "the best Christian in the world" and expressing what Jack Jones calls "an intense loathing for the musical heroes of his childhood: John Lennon and the Beatles." Lennon was replaced by Todd Rundgren as Mark's favorite rocker.

For several years Mark Chapman's discovery of religious faith led him to fruitful service on behalf of the YMCA. As a camp counselor, and subsequently assistant program director, he was popular with his young charges, who called him by his preferred nickname, Captain Nemo, borrowed from the protagonist of Jules Verne's *Twenty Thousand Leagues Under the Sea*. Nemo, the Latin word for "nothing," was an apt emblem of Mark's struggle with low self-esteem, and the children's admiration gave him the feeling that "those were the greatest days of [his] life. [He] was Nemo and everyone in camp loved [him]."

Early in 1975 Chapman was selected by the YMCA's international camp counselor program for summer work in Beirut, but Lebanon's civil war terminated his stay there in less than a month. Instead, Mark was offered employment at a YMCA-operated resettlement camp at Fort Chaffee, Arkansas, where he helped Vietnamese "boat people" refugees. The high point of the recognition that he received for his service was a handshake from President Gerald Ford.

It was at this point that Mark Chapman's life began an irreversible slide. Joining his fiancée, Jessica Blankenship, at Covenant College, a fundamentalist Presbyterian school in Tennessee, he fell into a depression and could not keep up with his classwork. After his return to Georgia, he sought the comfort of familiar work at the YMCA camp only to be faced with personal conflicts that challenged his memories of prestigious service in the past. He later told Jack Jones, "My YMCA identity fell apart, when I was stripped of that is when the clouds really started getting dark and I started slipping into an abyss that ended in murder, of someone I didn't even know." As a stopgap, Chapman took a job as a security guard, but, according to his fiancée's mother, "his personality began to change. He became quickly angry—just a trigger!" In January 1977, despairing of his prospects, Chapman fled to Hawaii, where, Jack Jones reports, he planned to take his life after a "last fling in paradise." After Mark later confessed his intentions to Jessica Blankenship in a telephone call from Honolulu and asked for assurance of her continuing love, she urged him to return home. He complied, but when the couple's Georgia reunion failed to restore their engagement, he returned to Honolulu, committed to his suicidal purpose. For him, however, death proved no easier than life, for the hose that he attached to the exhaust pipe of his automobile simply melted away.

Mark responded quickly to treatment at Castle Memorial Hospital for depression and in 1978 was on the move once again, this time on a tour around the world. On June 2, 1979, he married his travel agent, a Japanese American woman named Gloria Abe. Despite his new responsibilities, he remained unable to find stable employment. After jobs at Castle Memorial Hospital came to an end, he drifted into all-night security jobs that left him more free time than was good for him.

During his long hours at the Honolulu Public Library, his preoccupations with both John Lennon and the fictional Holden Caulfield deepened. On a library shelf he came upon Anthony Fawcett's *John Lennon: One Day at a Time*; the book persuaded him that Lennon, contrary to what he had said and sung, "was a successful man who had the world on a chain." He recalled to Jack Jones his sense of outrage that Lennon had "told us to imagine no possessions, and there he was, with millions of dollars and yachts and farms and country estates, laughing at people like me who had believed the lies and bought the records and built a big part of our lives around his music." During the same period Chapman reread *The Catcher in the Rye* for the first time since he was a teenager and found that Holden Caulfield, who dreamt of becoming a savior of children, gave him "a pseudo-identity." The blurring of Mark's personality with the two alter egos on whom he had become fixated left telltale signs that went unnoticed. Determined that he would win recognition as the Holden Caulfield of his generation, he inscribed a copy of *The Catcher in the Rye* to his wife, "To Gloria from Holden Caulfield," and his own copy, "From Holden Caulfield to Holden Caulfield."

Despite his disenchantment over John Lennon's affluent and showy lifestyle, he remained enmeshed in the superstar's personality. On October 23, 1980, when he checked out for the last time from his job as a maintenance man in a downtown Honolulu apartment building, he signed the register as "John Lennon"; he had also pasted Lennon's name over his uniform tag.

He translated his mixed feelings of attraction and repulsion into a plan to murder the Beatle hero.

With a brand-new .38 caliber revolver stowed in his checked baggage, Chapman flew home from Honolulu to New York City on October 29, bent on his deadly mission. To a girl he picked up while touring the city, he bragged, "Something is going to happen soon. You're going to hear about me." His anticipated celebrity, however, was blocked by the city's strict control over the sale of ammunition; he found that he could not acquire .38 caliber bullets without being licensed and bonded. In all innocence, an old Georgia friend, now a sheriff's deputy, solved his problem. Mark flew to Atlanta on the pretext of a sentimental journey and persuaded the deputy to supply him five cartridges with "real stopping power" in case he should be attacked on New York City's "frightening" streets; the bullets were hollow-pointed, designed to explode on impact.

Although all the components of murder were now in his hands, Mark stepped back from the brink of action. On November 12 he arrived in Honolulu, one day after having phoned Gloria from New York to confess that her love had saved him from carrying out his plan to kill Lennon. In the course of a month, however, his homicidal resolve strengthened again. He returned to New York on Saturday, December 6. Two days passed in fruitless watching at the entrance of the celebrity-favored Dakota apartment building at 72nd Street and Central Park West, where Lennon resided. But on Monday morning, December 8, Mark Chapman awoke early to try again. Before he left his hotel, he set out a display of mementos intended to catch the eyes of the police when they would search his room after the murder. Jack Jones describes the arrangement that he devised:

> Before leaving the hotel, Chapman had neatly arranged and left behind a curious assortment of personal items on top of the hotel dresser. In an orderly semicircle, he had laid out his passport, an eight-track tape of the music of Todd Rundgren, and his little Bible, open to The Gospel According to John (Lennon). He also left a letter from a former YMCA supervisor at Fort Chaffee, Arkansas, where, five years earlier, he had worked with refugees from the Vietnam War. Beside the letter were two photographs of himself surrounded by laughing Vietnamese children. At the center of the arrangement of personal effects, he had placed the small *Wizard of Oz* poster of Dorothy and the Cowardly Lion.

He took his station among the Lennon fans who watched outside the Dakota for sightings of their idol. His actions near the doorway reflected the odd mélange of his feelings toward the world-famous musician and activist. At first Chapman's love for Lennon seemed to take the upper hand. In the early afternoon he caught sight of Lennon's five-year-old son, Sean, escorted by his nanny. Jack Jones re-creates the scene:

> As he was introduced to John Lennon's son, Chapman stepped forward and uncurled the sweaty fingers of his right hand from around the chunk of steel. Sliding his hand carefully from the deep pocket of his coat, he knelt on one knee before Sean Lennon. He wrapped his fingers around the child's tiny hand.
>
> "I came all the way across the ocean from Hawaii and I'm honored to meet you," he said. The child stared at him blankly and sneezed.
>
> Chapman smiled.
>
> "You'd better take care of that runny nose," he said. "You wouldn't want to get sick and miss Christmas."

In the evening Mark's long wait was rewarded: he saw John Lennon and Yoko Ono leaving the Dakota entrance. As Chapman stood thunderstruck, Paul Goresh, a freelance photographer, reminded Mark of his announced intention to obtain the superstar's autograph on the latest Lennon-Ono album, *Double Fantasy,* which he had purchased the day before. Without speaking a word, Mark held out the album; Lennon laughed in acknowledgment of his fan's attachment and signed, "John Lennon. December, 1980." Thrilled to have acquired the collector's item, Mark offered Goresh $50 for a picture of his magic encounter with Lennon.

According to Jones's account, Mark did not wait for a report from the photographer's studio. A little before 11:00 o'clock that night, Lennon and Yoko Ono returned to the Dakota from a recording studio. When Lennon emerged from the limousine, Chapman, assuming a combat stance, rapidly fired four bullets into his target's back; the fifth shot went astray. Arrested as Lennon lay dying, Chapman told police officers, "I am the Catcher in the Rye." They bagged as evidence a copy of the Salinger novel that Mark had bought that morning; as he had previously done on his Hawaii copy, he had written an inscription "To Holden Caulfield from Holden Caulfield," but this time added below "This is my statement."

After forgoing his original plan to use his trial to publicize *The Catcher in the Rye,* Chapman pled guilty to second-degree murder and was sentenced to serve a term from twenty years to life in Attica prison. Before the disposition of his case, he was examined by a series of forensic psychiatrists. Dr. Naomi Goldstein, appointed by the court to pass on Chapman's competency to stand trial, reported that the defendant "had an insatiable need for attention and recognition . . . [and] grandiose visions of himself." He had avowed to her his mixed feelings about Lennon; he did not hate him, but thought he was a phony, just as he was portrayed in Anthony Fawcett's book. He added revealingly, "I admire him in a way. I wished someone would write a book about me."

Dr. Daniel Schwartz, on the basis of his examination of the defendant, had been prepared to opine at trial that Chapman was schizophrenic and also suffered from a "narcissistic personality disorder" causing him to crave attention and fame. Dr. Schwartz believed that the defendant was in the grips of a confusion with his victim's identity; he noted that Chapman, like Lennon, had married a woman of Japanese origin who was a few years older; had entered the rock star's name on a name tag and work log; and had given up his employment after learning that Lennon had become a househusband. Another defense expert, Dr. Richard Bloom, agreed that Chapman was schizophrenic and the victim of delusions of grandeur. According to Bloom's findings, as summarized by Jack Jones, Mark Chapman "was unable ever to unify the various elements of his personality into a cohesive and recognizable self."

At the sentencing hearing, District Attorney Allen Sullivan did not introduce any psychiatric testimony. In his speech he described Mark Chapman as a remorseless killer who "remains only interested in himself, his own well-being, what affects him, what's important to him at the particular moment." The defendant's "primary motive," Sullivan argued, was "personal aggrandizement, to draw attention to himself, to massage his own ego."

Chapman's only contribution to the proceedings was to read aloud a passage from *The Catcher in the Rye.*

Bibliographical Notes

The main factual sources for my discussion of the murder of John Lennon are Jack Jones, *Let Me Take You Down: Inside the Mind of Mark David Chapman, the Man Who Killed John Lennon* (New York: Villard, 1992), 250, 190, 124, 132, 137, 177, 195, 19, 31, 78, 75, 79–82; and Fenton Bresler, *Who Killed John Lennon?* (New York: St. Martin's, 1980), 125, 278.

In previous work, I have observed the likelihood that Mark Chapman, like the ancient Greek arsonist, Herostratos, committed his crime in pursuit of fame. See Albert Borowitz, *Terrorism for Self-Glorification: The Herostratos Syndrome* (Kent, Ohio: Kent State Univ. Press, 2005). Lutz Hübner makes a similar point in his play *The Orifice of the Heart: The Ballad of Herostratos Chapman* (1998).

Part Two

Crime in Music

9

Lamech, the Second Biblical Killer: A Song with Variations

Genesis records that Lamech, a fifth-generation descendant of Cain, took two wives, named Adah and Zillah. The terse reference to the world's first bigamy carried no moral assessment of the innovation in human relations; patriarchs before the Flood took up Lamech's practice, and King Solomon was reputed to have engaged in multiple marriage on a grand scale. Still, there were eventually dissenting voices in postbiblical literature of the ancient Jews. Strong reproof of primeval bigamy is made in the rabbinic commentary on Genesis in the *Midrash Rabbah* (perhaps compiled in the sixth century C.E.): "The men of the generation of the Flood used to act thus: each took two wives, one for procreation and the other for sexual gratification. The former would stay like a widow throughout her life, while the latter was given to drink a potion of roots, so that she should not bear, and then she sat before him like a harlot. . . . The proof of this is that Lamech took two wives."

The account in Genesis (4:17–22), however, belies the charge that Lamech married twice to separate procreation from sexual pleasure, for each of his wives bore him children: Adah had two sons with confusingly similar names, Jabal and Jubal; and Zillah was the mother of a son, Tubal-cain, and a daughter, Naamah. Each of Lamech's children was remarkable for creativity in cattle raising, arts, or sciences. Genesis relates that Jabal was "the ancestor of those who dwell in tents and amidst herds"; that Jubal was the forerunner of "all who play the lyre and pipe"; and that Tubal-cain "forged all implements of copper and iron." Naamah's accomplishments are not detailed in Genesis, but according to Louis Ginzberg, ancient Jewish tradition derived her name, "the lovely," from "the sweet sounds which she drew from the cymbals when she called the worshippers to pay homage to idols." Temples became a family enterprise, for "Jabal was the first among men to erect temples to idols, and Jubal invented the music sung and played therein."

In dark contrast to his children's honored achievements is the remembrance of Lamech as a pathfinder in crime. On the basis of his brief appearance in Genesis, he can be seen as the prototypical embodiment of inherited criminality (passing down from his ancestor Cain) and was also the first to vaunt the murderous use of the metal weapons perfected by his son Tubal-cain. To crown his infamy, Lamech is also recognized as the earliest multiple killer and the father of feuds.

Once Genesis has completed its introduction of Lamech, his wives, and children, the prose narrative breaks off abruptly and a poem takes up the thread. Known alternatively as "the Song of the Sword" or "the Song of Lamech," this jubilant outburst has been called the "first true example of biblical Hebrew style." And Lamech said to his wives,

> Adah and Zillah, hear my voice;
> O wives of Lamech, give ear to my speech.
> I have slain a man for wounding me,
> And a lad for bruising me.
> If Cain is avenged sevenfold,
> Then Lamech seventy-sevenfold.

E. A. Speiser, editor of the *Anchor Genesis,* notes that the poem "is generally viewed as the cry of a vengeful tribesman who has triumphed over his enemy" and speculates that, "if the song is tribal in origin, its ultimate source has to be sought outside historic Mesopotamia, possibly even to the south of Palestine." The *JPS* [Jewish Publication Society] *Torah Commentary* suggests that "the Song of Lamech probably originally belonged to a larger poetic composition about the exploits of this hero." Nahum M. Sarna, general editor of the *Commentary,* is attracted by the possibility that Lamech's words constitute his "taunts, threats, and boastings, which are of the kind customarily uttered in ancient times by those about to engage in combat," as in the story of David and Goliath.

However independent its origin may have been, the Song of the Sword, as inserted in Genesis, provides an essential link in the story of Cain and his descendants. The poem looks back to the punishment of Cain's crime and anticipates further escalating violence that lay ahead for the family line until it was ultimately swept away in the Flood with which God exacted retribution for "man's wickedness on earth."

Although Lamech's communication to his wives appears to reflect a key event in humanity's widening evil, Adah and Zillah must have been left bewildered by their husband's remarks unless he favored them with additional details that the Bible omits. Was Lamech boasting of his prowess in war? Calling into question Nahum Sarna's comparison of the Song of the Sword to the confrontation of David and Goliath, the text of Lamech's poem makes no reference to battle. There is, in fact, some adherence in interpretive literature to the theory that Lamech was confessing private acts of homicide. The "wounding" and "bruising" to which Lamech responded with lethal force may have been injuries suffered on a prior occasion, or Lamech may have acted in self-defense to ward off a current attack by an individual assailant. Sarna's commentary appears to favor the former of these two possibilities: "Alternatively, Lamech may be describing some incident that has already taken place in which he actually shed blood to avenge a previously inflicted wound."

The Song of the Sword also leaves unresolved the number of Lamech's victims. If, as many interpreters assert, Lamech claimed the lives of two victims, a "man" who had wounded him and a "lad" who had bruised him, he surpassed his ancestor Cain in villainy by becoming the biblical world's first serial killer. Sarna, however, observes that the poem is constructed on the basis of parallelism, that it features couplets in which the second line may either restate the first in different words or express an independent but related thought. For example, "wives of Lamech" in line 2 are synonymous with "Adah and Zillah" in line 1; yet, "Lamech" in line 6 is a person distinct from "Cain" in line 5, but the names are related through kinship. Sarna suggests that if "man" and "child" are synonymous, the two expressions may refer to a single foe, and that Lamech may be crowing: "This man, my antagonist, is a mere child in combat!"

The final couplet of the poem establishes an enigmatic comparison between the crimes of Lamech and of his ancestor Cain. As suggested by "the Song of the Sword," the alternative title given by tradition to Lamech's poem, the murderer's joy in his killings is enhanced by a sense of technological superiority, by his use of the metallic weapons invented by his son Tubal-cain. This supposition is confirmed by rabbinic commentary in the

Midrash Rabbah: "This man [Tubal-cain] perfected Cain's sin: Cain slew, yet lacked the weapons for slaying, whereas he was "the forger of every cutting instrument." Having surpassed Cain in weaponry and, very likely, in number of victims, Lamech asserted in his poem's finale that his life was entitled to even more heavily disproportionate protection against retaliation than was Cain's. When the exiled Cain expressed fear that anyone who met him in his wanderings might kill him, the Lord promised that "if anyone kills Cain, sevenfold vengeance shall be taken on him." Lamech boasts to his wives, "If Cain is avenged sevenfold, / Then Lamech seventy-sevenfold." Lamech sets an inflated value on his own life and appears to forecast that a future attack on him will provoke a feud that will spiral out of control. The immoderation of violent impulse is accompanied by religious blindness. It was not a human being but God who imposed a promise of manifold revenge as a shield to Cain; this protection was granted after the world's first murderer expressed his loneliness in having forfeited God's care. Lamech, unlike Cain, arrogated to himself and his line the authority to forgive his own crimes and ordained an even more disproportionate vengeance for any reprisals. A Christian sermon published online in 2002 characterized Lamech's sin as a usurpation of God's grace.

By the arrival of the Hellenistic Age, Jewish writers began to reflect variant postbiblical Lamech narratives. Historian Flavius Josephus, born in Jerusalem in 37 C.E., appraised grimly the violence and wildness of Cain's descendants: "even while Adam was alive, it came to pass that the posterity of Cain became exceedingly wicked, every one successively dying one after another more wicked than the former. They were intolerable in war, and vehement in robberies; and if anyone were slow to murder people, yet was he bold in his profligate behaviour, in acting unjustly and doing injuries for gain." Still, Josephus appears to exempt Lamech from this sweeping condemnation and to reject the confession of crime conveyed by the literal words of the Song of the Sword. What Lamech disclosed to his wives, Josephus recounts, was his foreknowledge that he was to be punished for Cain's murder of his brother Abel; the accuracy of this prediction was facilitated by Lamech's great skill "in matters of divine revelation." However, *The Biblical Antiquities of Philo,* a first-century C.E. work of an unknown Jewish author referred to as Pseudo-Philo, also exculpates Lamech of murder but only to tar his name with some unspeakable offenses against morality. Pseudo-Philo's version of the Song of the Sword proclaims: "Hear my voice, ye wives of Lamech, give heed to my precept:

for I have corrupted men for myself, and have taken sucklings from the breasts, that I might show my sons how to work evil."

Many nonbiblical sources from ancient times through the Middle Ages concur in another interpretation of what Lamech confessed to his wives, namely that he had caused the death of two relatives in a tragic hunting accident. Robert Graves and Raphael Patai summarize the Lamech narratives that fall into this pattern:

> Lamech was a mighty hunter and, like all others of Cain's stock, married two wives. Though grown old and blind, he continued to hunt, guided by his son Tubal Cain. Whenever Tubal Cain sighted a beast, he would direct Lamech's aim. One day he told Lamech: "I spy a head peeping above yonder ridge." Lamech drew his bow; Tubal Cain pointed an arrow which transfixed the head. But, on going to retrieve the quarry, he cried: "Father, you have shot a man with a horn growing from his brow!" Lamech answered: "Alas, he must be my ancestor Cain!", and struck his hands together in grief, thereby inadvertently killing Tubal Cain also.

The horn sighted by Tubal-cain was, of course, the "mark of Cain" God imbedded in the first murderer's forehead. In an essay entitled "Jewish Folklore: East and West," Louis Ginzberg cites a variant means of Cain's death: when Lamech's son and hunting guide "discerned something horned in the distance, he turned Lamech's arm upon it, and the creature fell dead." Ginzberg emphasizes two "genuinely folkloristic elements" in the story: "The horned Cain as well as the giant Lamech—who but a giant could crush a man to death?—are taken from the popular belief of Jews and Christians that the Cainites were monsters and giants."

One of the medieval Genesis commentaries exploring this version of the Lamech story was the work of Rashi (Rabbi Shlomo Yitzchaki) (1040–1105 C.E.). Here it is stated (in accord with the account in the *Midrash Tanchuma*) that Lamech's wives separated from him when they heard of his responsibility for the deaths of Cain and Tubal-cain. Lamech tried to appease them by arguing that he had acted inadvertently and without premeditation in shooting Cain and in mortally wounding his son and hunting guide, Tubal-cain. The spurned husband also made a self-serving interpretation of the divine promise that Cain, if murdered, would be "avenged sevenfold." Lamech explained to his spouses that the number seven referred

Lamech Killing Cain, illumination by Belbello da Pavia (active ca. 1430–1473), in the Codex Landau-Finaly (Visconti Hours), Biblioteca Nazionale, Florence. Credit: Scala Archives.

to the number of generations for which Cain's punishment for killing Abel was to be postponed. Lamech inferred from this divine leniency that his own case would be treated even more favorably: "If in the case of Cain who killed with premeditation the punishment was suspended for him until the seventh generation [when he died in the hunting calamity], in the case of myself who slew inadvertently, does it not necessarily follow that it should be suspended for me until many seven generations?"

Rashi, however, did not insist on the veracity of the hunting story because he observed, in all fairness, that it was at odds with a cosmic explanation provided in the *Midrash Rabbah.*

According to the *Midrash Rabbah,* Lamech's wives forswore their marital duties not because of any misdeed on his part but because the world was coming to an end. "Tomorrow a flood will come," they told him in chorus. "Are we to bear children for a curse?" God's wrath against His Creation is not my fault, Lamech answers. He turns the boast of the Song of the Sword into a rhetorical question: "Have I slain a man for my wounding—that wounds should come on his account! And a young man child for my bruising—that bruises should come upon me!" In simpler terms, Lamech is asking why, though innocent of violence, he should be "wounded" or "bruised" by denial of sexual relations. To allay his wives' fears of the Deluge, Lamech proposes that his guiltlessness should induce the Lord to withhold the destruction of the world: "Cain slew, yet judgment was suspended for him for seven generations; for me, who did not slay, surely judgment will wait seventy-seven generations." The egocentricity of this contention is breathtaking: Lamech suggests that because of his asserted innocence, God will suspend for seventy-seven generations His decreed annihilation of the sinful human race. The fallaciousness of Lamech's argument is noted in a rabbinic citation included in the Midrash: "This is a reasoning of darkness: for if so, whence is the Holy One, blessed be He, to exact His bond of debt [i.e., to enforce his judgment levied against all humanity]?"

Even if the Midrash is justified in rejecting Lamech as a self-appointed redeemer of humanity, this version of his tale brings him close to the experience of the modern age. Those who have lived under the shadow of nuclear catastrophe and terrorist attack can feel affinity with the man who tried to pacify his wives' fears about the imminence of a Deluge.

Lamech and Two Prophets

The Song of Lamech received extremely divergent revisions in the eighteenth and nineteenth centuries by prophets of two revealed offshoots of Christianity. In Swedish mystic Emanuel Swedenborg's *Heavenly Secrets* (1749), Lamech's song does not describe actual events but is to be understood as an allegorical representation of religious doctrine. By contrast, Mormonism's founder Joseph Smith, in *The Book of Moses,* not only accepts murder by Lamech as literal fact but darkens the crime by relating it to a prior Satanic oath.

The Swedenborg Foundation describes Swedenborg's *Heavenly Secrets* as a "systematized explanation of the spiritual import contained within the imagery, fable and history of the Old Testament." In his introduction to the work, Swedenborg tells of the divine origin of the revelations he received regarding the "spiritual and heavenly things" underlying the literal words of the scriptures: "Of the Lord's divine mercy it has been granted me now for some years to be constantly and uninterruptedly in company with spirits and angels, hearing them speak and in turn speaking with them. . . . I have been instructed in regard to the different kinds of spirits; the state of souls after death; hell, or the lamentable state of the unfaithful; heaven, or the blessed state of the faithful; and especially in regard to the doctrine of faith which is acknowledged in the universal heaven." In Swedenborg's teachings, a crucial process that prepares the way for acceptance of true faith is the emptying of an outworn faith from the afflicted soul. This course of spiritual transformation is accomplished by what Swedenborg refers to as "vastation." Swedenborg teaches that a church "in process of time departs from the true faith and finally ends in no faith. When there is none it is said to be 'vastated.' . . . The reason why the new light or 'morning' does not shine forth until the church is vastated, is that the things of faith and of charity have been commingled with things profane; and so long as they remain in this state it is impossible for anything of light or charity to be insinuated." The Song of Lamech, in Swedenborg's reading, is not a tale of double murder, as a literal reading would suggest, but a parable of the arrival at a state of faithlessness or vastation: "That by 'Lamech' is signified vastation, or that there was no faith, is evident from the . . . verses . . . in which it is said that he 'slew a man to his wounding, and a little one to his hurt'; for there by a 'man' is meant faith, and by a 'little one' or 'little child,' charity." In this interpretation, typical of Swedenborg's symbolic reading of the biblical text, the loss of two lives comes to mean the annihilation of adulterated faith and charity to make ready for the light to shine forth from a "New Church."

Joseph Smith, first prophet of the Mormon Church, recorded in *The Book of Moses* revelations made to him in 1830. In the words of God, spoken "unto Moses at a time when Moses was caught up into an exceedingly high mountain," both Cain and his descendant Lamech are denounced as creatures of Satan. Cain "loved Satan more than God" and took a secret oath to do the archfiend's bidding. In return, Satan promised that very day to deliver Abel into his hands. Swearing his obedience, Cain took the occult appellation of Master Mahan: "Truly I am Master Mahan," Cain said. "I am the master of this great secret, that I may murder and get gain." Glorying in his wickedness, he murdered Abel and defended his crime before God with the words "Satan tempted me because of my brother's flocks." Lamech followed the example of his ancestor in both diabolism and murder. He entered into "a covenant with Satan, after the manner of Cain, wherein he became Master Mahan, master of that great secret which was administered unto Cain by Satan." Lamech's great-grandfather, Irad, learned of the infernal oaths of Cain and Lamech and began to reveal their secret to the "sons of Adam." In anger over the disclosure, Lamech killed Irad, "not like unto Cain [who murdered] his brother Abel, for the sake of getting gain, but he slew him for the oath's sake."

Joseph Smith's revelation attributes this new family violence to a "secret combination" that was operative "from the days of Cain." The Lord "cursed Lamech, and his house, and all them that had covenanted with Satan." Cain and malefactors in his line had not kept God's commandments, and their works were "abominations [that] began to spread among all the sons of man." *The Book of Moses* substitutes for the Song of the Sword Lamech's confessions to his wives of his pledge to Satan and the murder of Irad. Shocked by what they heard, they "rebelled against him, and declared these things abroad, and had not compassion." As a result, "Lamech was despised, and cast out, and came not among the sons of men, lest he should die." It was in the misdeeds of Cain and Lamech that the "works of darkness began to prevail among the sons of men," bringing God's "sore curse" on the Earth.

Poetry and Drama of Lamech through the Centuries

> An old song vexes my ear,
> But that of Lamech is mine.
> —Lord Tennyson, *Maud*

When the Lamech theme has been pursued in poetry or drama, a striking feature of all the works is what they omit. Like the Genesis passage that originated Lamech's story, as well as the commentaries and legends it inspired, the subsequent poems and plays of Lamech do not elaborate the circumstances or motivation of the vengeful acts suggested by a literal reading of the Song of the Sword. Perhaps the very minimalism of the biblical portrait has inhibited imaginative retouching. Murray H. Lichtenstein, in an essay on biblical poetry, has accurately characterized Lamech's song as a "tantalizingly terse vignette" that "succeeds admirably in drawing with precision and economy the emotional contours of an outspoken personality who would have otherwise been relegated to a silent slot in the genealogy that precedes the passage."

Perhaps the notion of Lamech as an "outspoken personality" is the key to his impenetrability. When his heart is examined, what lies there for certain—except braggadocio? William Ian Miller, in his study of retaliation, *Eye for an Eye,* notes that we must trust the veracity of Lamech's exploits "to his own boast to his wives, who for all we know might have been rolling their eyes." Due to lack of insight into Lamech as killer, the poets and dramatists have adopted other strategies. Medieval authors have often chosen the legendary theme of Lamech's killing of Cain. More recent works have focused on such motifs as rivalry between Lamech's children and the end of the curse that afflicted Cain and his descendants.

The long scriptural poems in Old English that were for centuries attributed to Caedmon (fl. 670) are now regarded to be of unknown authorship. A poem based on Genesis revises the biblical original of the Song of the Sword to identify Cain as Lamech's victim: "Then to his two beloved wives, Adah and Zillah, Lamech rehearsed a tale of shame: 'I have struck down a kinsman unto death! I have defiled my hands with the blood of Cain! I smote down Enoch's father, slayer of Abel, and poured his blood upon the ground. Full well I know that for that mortal deed shall come God's seven-fold vengeance. With fearful torment shall my deed of death and murder be requited, when I go hence.'" The poet does not specify whether Cain was the victim of a hunting accident, as in the noncanonical tradition of antiquity, or whether he was struck down willfully. Murder, however, seems to be on the poet's mind, for his Lamech believes that the killing will subject him to "God's seven-fold vengeance" that was assured by the protective mark of Cain.

Edmund Reiss has noted that a few of the medieval cycle plays dealing with Noah's ark and the Deluge insert a scene showing Lamech killing Cain. Reiss pays particular attention to the "version of the Noah story contained in the Middle English *Ludus Coventriae [The Coventry Play]*— now generally called the N-Town Cycle." In a brief interlude of *The Coventry Play* (edited by K. S. Black), blind old Lamech, led to the hunt by a youthful guide, recalls his past prowess in archery and asks the boy to guide his hand so that he can show the skill that he retains. He shoots Cain, mistaking him for a beast, and beats the guide to death with his bow. Fearing divine wrath, he flees the scene of the double killing.

> For death of Cain I shall have sevenfold
> More pain than he had that Abel did slay.
> These two men's deaths full sore bought shall be.
> Upon all my blood God will avenge this deed.
> Wherefore, sore weeping, hence will I flee
> And look where I may best my head soon hide.

As these lines echo, Noah and his family enter the ark. Noah mourns the "dreadful flood" that will punish the sins of man's "wild mood," sinful living, and lechery.

St. Jerome linked Lamech's bigamy with his two homicides as analogous instances of excesses unrestrained by morality. In a letter to Salvina, a court lady, he wrote in 400 C.E.: "The accursed and blood-stained Lamech, descended from the stock of Cain, was the first to make out of one rib two wives; and the seedling of digamy [a legal second marriage] then planted was altogether destroyed by the doom of the deluge." Uninfluenced by the Church father, however, Geoffrey Chaucer repeatedly satirized Lamech's two marriages while overlooking the double murder imputed to him by Genesis. The Wife of Bath, in the prologue to her tale in *The Canterbury Tales,* is an expert on marriage, having been led to the altar five times since she was twelve. She defends her inclination to wedlock with scriptural references to polygamy, including the fashion-setting example of Lamech: "In sooth, I will not keep me chaste wholly; when my husband is departed from the world, anon some other Christian man shall wed me. For then, the apostle says, I am free, a God's name, to wed where I list. He says that it is no sin to be wedded; better it is to be wedded than to burn. What reck I though folk speak shame of cursed Lamech and his bigamy? Well I wot Abraham was an holy man and eke Jacob, so far forth as I know, and each of them had more wives than two, and eke many another holy man." The example of Lamech is also well-known to a learned falcon in "The Squire's Tale"; the talking bird refers to a feathered suitor who had a "bearing so like a gentle lover, so ravished with bliss, as it seemed, that never Jason, nor Paris of Troy . . . nor any man else since Lamech was, who first of all began to love two."

The most amusing reference to Lamech in Chaucer's work is found in the unfinished poem "Anelida and Arcite." There the poet proclaims Lamech, rather than his shepherd son Jabal, to be the inventor of tents. Instead of serving as mobile homes for the tenders of flocks, the poem suggests that tents were originally devised to conceal Lamech's trysts: "Lamech was the first patriarch who loved two women, and lived in bigamy; and unless men lie, he first invented tents."

In *Lamech, ou Les Descendants de Caïn,* a French verse drama by Charles Brifaut (poet, dramatist, opera librettist, and member of the French Academy), the curse of Cain continues to play itself out in the destinies of Lamech and sons Tubal-cain and Jabal. Although capable of losing his temper, the Lamech imagined by Brifaut makes no allusion to the violent events mirrored by the Song of the Sword. Having reached old age, Lamech may have forgotten the bloody confrontations he bragged about in his youth, or perhaps they never happened.

Early in the first act of the play, Lamech's wife, Noéma, who combines his two biblical spouses, reveals a grievous loss early in her marriage. An unknown elderly kidnapper stole her infant son, Tubal-cain, from her arms, overcoming her defensive struggles with the oracular words: "Stop! Marked by the deadly seal, this child belongs to me. Tremble lest he remain with you." This enigmatic warning establishes a theme of secret interplay between two mysterious figures: the kidnapper, who will ultimately reveal himself to be the wandering Cain, and the stolen child, who, unaware of his name and birth, will grow up to be a warrior and sword forger who is called Coreb. The meaning of the oracle pronounced at the time of the abduction will be revealed only when its disclosure cannot avert disaster.

Mirroring the primal discord between Cain and Abel, a potentially deadly quarrel arises between Jabal and his unrecognized brother. Both of the young men are in love with Lamech's niece, Saphira. Jabal grew up with Saphira and regarded her as a sister before she became his beloved. Although the match received the blessing of Jabal's parents, Coreb (Tubal-cain) objects furiously. Having defeated the attack of Abel's kinsmen on Lamech's domain, Coreb claims Saphira's hand as his reward and threatens to murder Lamech and Jabal when they persist in making arrangements for the shepherd's wedding.

Cain appears as an old man emerging from a forest; he is dressed in a tiger's skin, and long hair disguises a part of his features. He has initial success in dissuading Coreb from taking precipitous revenge; Coreb is frightened because he thinks he sees in the old man "the living anger of the Almighty." Jabal reacts to the newcomer more in curiosity than fear, asking him to reveal his face, and identifies the community as the "inheritance of Cain." The stranger is touched by the sympathy of Jabal and Saphira for the world's first murderer, but the pursuit of a jealous God is unrelenting: the water and dates that the young people offer him "rebel."

Despite Cain's intervention, the dangerous rivalry of Lamech's sons mounts in intensity, and Coreb pursues his murder plans. Cain warns the young soldier of the unforgiving fate of murderers and, pressing him in his arms, expresses the wish: "If only some friendly voice, by a cry of terror, had, / When I was about to strike, restrained my fury." By degrees, the old man reveals to Coreb (Tubal-cain) the secret of his birth in the accursed line of murderers and the reason for his kidnapping.

I approach, I observe, and my alarmed eye
Sees crime expressed in the forehead of the infant;
His features prophesied his dark destiny,
I snatch him from the arms of his astonished mother.

Astounded by the gradual revelation of his family ties, Coreb (once again restored to his identity as Tubal-cain), recedes from his murder plans, but only for the moment. Noéma finds the corpse of her husband, Lamech, lying in the woods, the victim of Tubal-cain. The biblical swordsman has died by his son's sword. Cain, in his final speech, foresees that ever-increasing crime will lead humanity to extinction in the Flood.

> From now on we will see, surpassing each other in crime,
> One sacrificed by the other, both executioners and victims,
> Mortals rushing into this disastrous field
> Until the day, fatal day when on these wretched humans
> God unleashing the floods of his slow vengeance,
> All will die engulfed under an immense storm.
> But, bearing the future of a new universe,
> The ark where Noah is enclosed rests on the seas.

Rudyard Kipling, a Freemason since he joined an Indian Lodge in 1885, devoted some of his fiction and poems to Masonic themes. He was aware that all three of Lamech's sons have been celebrated as discoverers of the sciences in the "Legend of the Craft," with which the traditional history of Masonry begins. Kipling's poem "Jubal and Tubal Cain" sings of the sibling rivalry between two of Lamech's sons, Jubal the musician and Tubal-cain. The poem recalls the feud in which Lamech is sometimes said to have taken the lives of two foemen with weapons invented by Tubal-cain. That deadly conflict, Kipling suggests, was no more bitter than the clash between fraternal temperaments.

> Jubal sang of the golden years,
> When wars and wounds shall cease—
> But Tubal fashioned the hand-flung spears
> And showèd his neighbours peace.
> New—new as the Nine-point-Two [the largest gun carried by a heavy
>   cruiser],
> Older than Lamech's slain [victims]—
> Roaring and loud is the feud avowed
> Twix' Jubal and Tubal Cain!

Even though the two creative brothers have apparently not inherited their ancestors' murderous instincts, they appear to share the fierce competitiveness of Cain and Lamech.

The murder charges against Lamech are expunged in George Eliot's narrative poem "The Legend of Jubal," published in 1870. In Cain's "young city," established by him in exile, "none had heard of Death save him, the founder." In Eliot's telling, it becomes Lamech's tragic lot to introduce death to the community after generations of innocence; by pure accident he takes the life of one of his children.

> . . . hurling stones in mere athletic joy,
> Strong Lamech struck and killed his fairest boy,
> And tried to wake him with the tenderest cries,
> And fetched and held before the glazèd eyes
> The things they best had loved to look upon;
> But never glance or smile or sigh he won.

As the "generations" looked on in amazement, ancient Cain explained the unprecedented calamity that they had witnessed.

> "He will not wake;
> This is the endless sleep, and we must make
> A bed deep down for him beneath the sod;
> For know, my sons, there is a mighty God
> Angry with all man's race, but most with me.
> I fled from out His land in vain! 'tis He
> Who came and slew the lad. . . ."

In this passage Cain makes a thoroughgoing defense of Lamech's guiltlessness. The world's first murderer, living on among several generations of his progeny, has never before disclosed human mortality, the murder of Abel, or the causative link between violence and death. The impermanence of life is due to "Jehovah's will, and He is strong; / I thought the way I travelled was too long / For Him to follow me; my thought was vain!"

In "The Song of Lamech," Victorian poet Arthur Hugh Clough devised a comforting backstory for Lamech's biblical outcry—a narrative of forgiveness and reconciliation among Cain, his parents, and his murdered brother, Abel. The family peace lifts the curse of Cain and gives promise that Lamech's violent acts will not initiate a new chain of reprisal.

The first lines of Clough's poem echo the beginning of the Genesis poem: "Hearken to me, ye mothers of my tent; / Ye wives of Lamech, hearken to my speech." Immediately thereafter, however, it becomes plain that Lamech will not address his spouses alone. "Adah," he asks, "let

Jubal [conflated here with his brother Jabal] hither lead his goats"; Tubal Cain is to "hush the forge," his sister Naamah is to ply her wheel nearby, and Jubal is to touch his instrument's string before his father begins to speak. What Lamech has to say concerns the entire family: "Hear ye my voice, beloved of my tent, / Dear ones of Lamech, listen to my speech."

Lamech's tale begins by recalling how Adam and Eve attempted to persuade Cain not to go into exile after the murder of Abel. The contrite Eve acknowledged that if she had cursed Cain she had sinned, and Adam joined their forgiveness to that he deemed proffered by the dead Abel: "He that is gone forgiveth, we forgive: / Rob not thy mother of two sons at once; / My child, abide with us and comfort us." Cain brooded on his parents' entreaty through the night, but when the sun rose he announced that he must go into exile just as his parents were banished from Eden.

Cain's "years were multiplied," and his heirs reached several generations. In old age he lived alone, and once, at nightfall, he met Adam in the field. His father asked him a probing question: "My son, hath God not spoken to thee?" Cain replied that his dreams were "double, good and evil," bringing "terror to [his] soul by night, and agony by day." Abel's daytime apparition stood as "A dead black shade, and speaks not neither looks, / Nor makes me any answer when I cry. . . ." In "visions of a deeper sleep," however,

Abel, as whom we knew, yours once and mine,
Comes with a free forgiveness in his face,
Seeming to speak, solicitous for words,
And wearing ere he go the old, first look
Of unsuspecting, unforeboding love.

Cain told Adam that the pardoning vision appeared three nights before, and his father responded that on the very same night he saw Abel in his sleep. Abel asked him to visit Cain in his land of exile and to tell his brother that Abel wished to see him. Abel's phantom further enjoined Adam to "lay thou thy hand, / My father, on his head that he may come; / Am I not weary, Father, for this hour?" Adam responded with a magical touch upon the head of Cain, who "bowed down, and slept, and died." A deep sleep fell on Adam, and "in his slumber's deepest he beheld, / Standing before the gate of Paradise / With Abel, hand in hand, our father Cain."

Having finished his story of ancestral reconciliation, Lamech returns to the words of the Song of the Sword. Lamech's two killings are confessed, but, as in the King James Version, have not been committed in retaliation for prior injuries; it is Lamech's own homicides that have caused him "wounding" and "hurt." Moreover, unlike the Song of the Sword, in either the traditional Hebrew text or the King James translation, Clough's poem does not end on Lamech's warning of disproportionate revenge against any foes who may seek to punish him. Instead, Lamech assures his family that the safety and rest granted at last to Cain will ensure the future security of Lamech and his line.

> Hear ye my voice, Adah and Zillah, hear;
> Ye wives of Lamech, listen to my speech.
> Though to his wounding did he slay a man,
> Yea, and a young man to his hurt he slew,
> Fear not ye wives nor sons of Lamech fear:
> If unto Cain was safety given and rest,
> Shall Lamech surely and his people die?

It is in these words of peace that Arthur Clough takes leave of the Lamech tradition.

Bibliographical Notes

For the Genesis text and commentary, I relied principally on *JPS* [Jewish Publication Society] *Torah Commentary: Genesis, the Traditional Hebrew Text with the New JPS Translation,* commentary by Nahum M. Sarna (Philadelphia: Jewish Publication Society, 1989), 36–39, 38 ("first true example of Hebrew biblical style"). Other sources for text, commentary, targums, and apocrypha include: *Midrash Rabbah,* vol. 1, ed. and trans. H. Freedman and Maurice Simon (London: Soncino Press, 1951), 194–95; *The Anchor Bible: Genesis,* intro., trans., and notes E. A. Speiser (Garden City, N.Y.: Doubleday, 1964), 37; *Chumash with Targum, Onkelos, Haphtaroth and Rashi's Commentary Bereshith (Genesis),* trans. A. M. Silbermann, with M. Rosenbaum (Jerusalem: Silbermann Family, 1984–85); 19–21; *Metsudah Midrash Tanchuma: Bereishis I (Genesis),* ed. Yaakov Y. H. Pupko, trans. and ann. Avrohom Davis (Lakewood, N.J.: Israel Book Shop, 2005); 58–61; *Targum Onkelos to Genesis,* trans. Moses Aberbach and Bernard Grossfeld (New York: Ktav Publishing House, 1982); 44–46; *Targum Pseudo-Jonathan,* trans. with intro. and notes Michael Maher (Collegeville, Minn.: Liturgical Press, 1992); 34–35; *The Book of Jubilees: or, The Little Genesis,* trans. Robert Henry Charles (Berwick, Maine: Ibis Press, 2005), 56.

Lamech's song draws "contours of an outspoken personality," wrote Murray H. Lichtenstein, in "Biblical Poetry," in *Back to the Sources: Reading the Classic Jewish Texts,* ed. Barry W. Holtz (New York: Touchstone, 1984), 119–20.

In examining Hebrew myths I turned to Louis Ginzberg's *The Legends of the Jews,* vol. 1 (Baltimore: John Hopkins Univ. Press, 1998), 117–18; and his "Jewish Folklore: East and West," in *On Jewish Law and Lore* (Cleveland: Meridian Books, 1962), 61–62, wherein he states: "English, French, Italian, and Spanish artists vied with one another to depict the widely spread legend of the blind Lamech going to hunt under the guidance of his son Tubal Cain." Also valuable in my research was Robert Graves and Raphael Patai, *Hebrew Myths: The Book of Genesis* (Garden City, N.Y.: Doubleday, 1964), 108.

Sources of classical literature valuable in this study are Flavius Josephus, *Jewish Antiquities* (Ware, Hertfordshire: Wordsworth Editions, 2006), 11; Philo Judaeus, "Questions and Answers on Genesis, I," in *Works,* trans. C. D. Yonge (Peabody, Mass.: Hendrickson, 1993), 807; [Pseudo-Philo,] *The Biblical Antiquities of Philo,* trans. M. R. James (London: Society for Promoting Christian Knowledge, 1917), 78–79.

Two prophets of eighteenth- and nineteenth-century offshoots of Christianity modify the Lamech tradition: Emanuel Swedenborg, *Heavenly Secrets (Arcana Caelestia),* vol. 1 (New York: Swedenborg Foundation, 1967), 248–50; and Joseph Smith, "The Book of Moses," in *The Pearl of Great Price* (Salt Lake City, Utah: Church of Jesus Christ of Latter-Day Saints, 1928), 1, 12–14.

Lamech's story appears in centuries of poetry and drama: [Caedmon,] "Genesis Book XVIII," http://poemhunter.com (accessed Sept. 17, 2006; site discontinued); *Ludus Coventriae: or, The Plaie Called Corpus Christi,* Cotton Ms. Vespasian D. VIII, ed. K. S. Block (London: Oxford Univ. Press, 1974), xv, 39–43; Edmund Reiss, "The Story of Lamech and Its Place in Medieval Drama," *Comitatus: A Journal of Medieval and Renaissance Studies* 2 (1972): 35; Geoffrey Chaucer, *The Complete Poetical Works of Geoffrey Chaucer,* ed. John S. P. Tatlock and Percy MacKaye (New York: Macmillan, 1955), 157–58, 238–50, 356–61; Charles Brifaut, *Lamech, ou Les Descendans de Cain (1820),* in *Oeuvres de M. Charles Brifaut,* vol. 4 (Paris: Diard, 1858), 295–385, 302, 347, 349, 384; Rudyard Kipling, "Jubal and Tubal Cain," in *Rudyard Kipling's Verse* (Garden City, N.Y.: Doubleday, 1940), 555; George Eliot, "The Legend of Jubal," in *The Spanish Gypsy, The Legend of Jubal, and Other Poems, Old and New* (New York: Thomas Nelson, 1915), 383–425, 386, 388–89; Arthur Hugh Clough, "The Song of Lamech," in *The Poems of Arthur Hugh Clough* (Oxford, England: Oxford Univ. Press, 1968), 50–53.

The cited Christian sermon on Lamech's usurpation of God's Grace is "Lamech: The Biblical second murderer and the usurpation of Grace," http:/www.maxpages.com/oreoblues/Lamech (accessed Oct. 30, 2002; site discontinued).

I have also quoted from William Ian Miller, *Eye for an Eye* (New York: Cambridge Univ. Press, 2006), 24 (Lamech's wives "might have been rolling their eyes").

10

Gilbert and Sullivan on Corporation Law: Utopia, Limited *and the* Panama Canal Frauds

Whenever the name "Gilbert" was mentioned to the president of an American corporation in the late twentieth century, he would likely have thought of the brothers Lewis and John and wondered what shareholder proposals they might be preparing for the forthcoming annual meeting. However, the title of corporate gadfly extraordinaire could, with equal justice, be awarded to quite another Gilbert, W. S. Gilbert of the operatic partnership of Gilbert and Sullivan. In the relatively little-known opera *Utopia, Limited,* which appeared at the Savoy Theatre in 1893, Gilbert delivered a sharply satirical assault on business corporations (which the English call "companies"), and particularly on the basic corporate concept of limited liability. The opera sketches the development of a utopian society that organizes itself, its ruler, and all its citizens as limited liability companies under the English Companies Act of 1862.

The theme of *Utopia, Limited* has puzzled its critics and received strange evaluations. W. A. Darlington, in his *The World of Gilbert and Sullivan,* makes the suggestion (which he cautiously terms "a guess") that "Gilbert, not being in any sense a businessman, had never had any clear notion what a limited-liability company was" until shortly before he wrote *Utopia.* In light of his celebrated partnership disputes with Sullivan, Gilbert may be denied a businessman's standing only under the most subjective conception of that calling, but surely Darlington would not have us forget that the author of *Utopia* was a lawyer.

It is apparent from Hesketh Pearson's biography that Gilbert's career at the bar was spectacularly unsuccessful. It lasted four years and produced about twenty clients and a total income of £100. His difficulties seem to be fairly represented by his first brief, the defense of a female pickpocket, who, on being sentenced to a prison term, "threw a boot at his head and continued to criticize his personal character until removed from the court." The memories of this case are undoubtedly responsible for Gilbert's little gem, the short story "My Maiden Brief" (1890). In that story, the fledgling barrister, Horace Penditton, prepares for the trial of his first client, who filched a purse on an omnibus, by trying out a fanciful line of defense on Felix Polter, a barrister who occupies neighboring chambers in the Inner Temple. When Penditton appears in court, he is shocked to find that his opponent is none other than Polter, who calmly proceeds to anticipate all his defenses in opening the prosecution's case to the jury. When Penditton at the end of the story contrasts Polter's future with his own, we may be hearing a cri de coeur of Gilbert himself: "He is now a flourishing Old Bailey counsel, while I am as briefless as ever."

Although Gilbert's years as a lawyer were few, he had a very active and lifelong career as a client. In addition to his disputes with Sullivan and D'Oyly Carte over the expense of new carpets at the Savoy Theatre and a defamation suit against a newspaper, he filled his private hours with threats of litigation over grievances real and trivial. If his correspondence with an adversary took an unsatisfactory turn, he was likely to suggest that future letters be addressed to his solicitor. However, it is to his credit that he rounded out his functions as lawyer and client with able and compassionate service as a justice of the peace.

It is odd that neither Gilbert's contemporaries nor his biographers seem to have taken him seriously as a critic of business law and morality. Doubt seems always to arise as to whether Gilbert had strong roots in the real world. Of course, we have always enjoyed the game of matching Gilbert characters with eminent and lesser Victorians, but there has been no agreement that Gilbert was engaged by the social issues that enveloped the individual figures he found suitable for caricature. His biographer, Hesketh Pearson, ventures a psychological explanation for Gilbert's preoccupation with fairyland and fantasy, believing that Gilbert's childhood, spent with incompatible and often feuding parents, left him "an internal discomfort, a desire to see things as they are not, born of his early contact with an unpleasant actuality." Gilbert, however, had a perfectly pragmatic justification for his specialization in fairies. In his fairy tale "The Wicked World" (1890), he explained his choice of theme. He did not write of fashionable life because he knew nothing of fashion; nor did he write a medieval romance because this would require too much research (which Gilbert detested and preferred to call "cramming"). Gilbert noted the possible objection by an acute reader that if the author knew nothing of fashionable life, he must know still less about fairies. He offered a reply that is unanswerable: "Exactly. I know nothing at all about fairies—but then neither do you."

Perhaps the fantastic settings of Gilbert's plots have obscured his interest in legal issues. In some instances the reluctance of drama critics and audiences to listen to his more serious voice impeded his forays into criticism of prevailing legal principles. This was clearly his fate when he attempted to deal in his works with controversies in the field of criminal law. In Gilbert and Sullivan's *Iolanthe,* as first performed in 1882, the young shepherd Strephon, on admission to Parliament, delivered a speech attributing crime to circumstances of birth and upbringing:

Take a wretched thief
   Through the City sneaking,
Pocket handkerchief
   Ever, ever seeking:
What is he but I
   Robbed of all my chances—
Picking pockets by
   Force of circumstances?
I might be as bad—
   As unlucky, rather—
If I'd only had
   Fagin for a father!

Leslie Baily notes that the critic of the *Times of London* attacked Gilbert's expression of anger, "a passion altogether out of place in a fairy opera." The offending song was later cut from *Iolanthe.*

Gilbert's final dramatic work, the one-act play *The Hooligan,* produced in 1911, the last year of his life, was a completely serious treatment of capital punishment. Inspired by his fascination with the celebrated Crippen murder trial of 1910, Gilbert's play presented the last moments of a condemned murderer in his prison cell. The criminal is reprieved from hanging only to die of heart failure occasioned by the agony of waiting for death. Some of the spectators who expected laughs from Gilbert were perplexed and hissed.

Gilbert's literary reflection of his interest in criminal law is pretty much limited to the two examples given above (unless we are also to refer to his portrait of that great penologist, the Mikado of Japan). However, throughout the pages of his opera librettos are many signs of his perennial absorption in the behavior of corporations and businessmen. It is likely that his contemporaries cared as little for his views on business as they did for his assessments of criminal law. If we are to follow their pattern by assuming that Gilbert's comments on business morality have no application to our own time, we will probably be drawing on some false feeling of comfort.

Gilbert's first satire on corporations appeared appropriately in the very first opera he wrote with Sullivan, *Thespis* (1871). In this opera, Thespis, the manager of a theatrical troupe performing for the Olympian gods, sings the earliest Gilbert and Sullivan patter song, which lampoons the chairman of a railroad's board of directors who undermined his own authority and ruined his company by being too affable to company employees. I suppose that even the most democratic of executives would feel that the chairman went to extremes in his personnel policy:

> Each Christmas Day he gave each stoker
> A silver shovel and a golden poker,
> He'd button-hole flowers for the ticket sorters,
> And rich Bath-buns for the outside porters.
> He'd mount the clerks on his first-class hunters,
> And he built little villas for the road-side shunters . . .

The employees, surprised by the chairman's favors, assumed that his behavior was due to an odd quirk of humor rather than generosity and attempted to respond in kind by diverting any train on which he happened to be riding. The employees' vein of practical joking appeared to please the chairman more than the railroad's customers or shareholders.

> This pleased his whim and seemed to strike it,
> But the general Public did not like it,
> The receipts fell, after a few repeatings,
> And he got it hot at the annual meetings . . .

Undeterred by shareholder pressure, the chairman continued to indulge the employees in their merry pranks, with the result of business failure for himself and the investors: "The shareholders are all in the work'us [workhouse], / And he sells pipe-lights in the Regent Circus."

This first corporation song of Gilbert's is obviously less concerned with business practice than with an important tenet of Gilbert's conservative personality, namely, that excessive egalitarianism is fatal to established order. However, the song of Thespis also reveals two points that are crucial to an understanding of Gilbert's lasting interest in corporations. The lyrics show first his tendency to connect observations on corporate administration with theatrical management, a field in which he was to spend his life and where he was to encounter a great deal of difficulty in reconciling the conflicting interests of manager, investor, and employee. A second characteristic theme that the early song shows in germination is Gilbert's emphasis on the responsibility of corporate management to the public, including those whose investments they have called on and those with whom they do business.

Eleven years later, in Gilbert's great libretto for *Iolanthe,* business practice had become the stuff of nightmare, though of a comic turn. The lord chancellor, in his celebrated nightmare aria, recalls a dream in which a distinctly small fellow with a Protean inclination to change identities harangues a group of sailors on a new financing he is pushing. The promoter, who appears successively as an attorney and an eleven-year-old boy, describes the purpose of the financing in terms that are recalled by the delirious chancellor:

It's a scheme of devices, to get at low prices all goods from cough
    mixtures to cables
(Which tickled the sailors), by treating retailers as though they were
    all vegetables—
You get a good spadesman to plant a small tradesman (first take off his
    boots with a boot-tree),
And his legs will take root, and his fingers will shoot, and they'll
    blossom and bud like a fruit-tree . . .
The shares are a penny, and ever so many are taken by Rothschild and
    Baring,
And just as a few are allotted to you, you awake with a shudder
    despairing.

Only the timely waking of the chancellor has saved him from a disastrous investment. However, in spite of our regulatory advances, the sales techniques of the undersized promoter are not unlike those of present-day "penny stock" merchants, in whose sales pitch the projected use of proceeds may be less important than the general impression that the venture is new and that, in any event, there is likely to be some opportunity for movement in the stock when the initial price is low.

In the figure of the Duke of Plaza-Toro in *The Gondoliers* (1889), Gilbert introduced a man who more than compensated for his doubtful military talents with a real appreciation of the opportunities afforded by modern business. The duke and his worthy spouse found considerable profit in selling their aristocratic endorsements of worthless products and securities. As the duke puts it,

> Those pressing prevailers,
> The ready-made tailors,
>   Quote me as their great double-barrel—
>
> I allow them to do so,
> Though Robinson Crusoe
>   Would jib at their wearing apparel—
>
> I sit, by selection,
> Upon the direction
>   Of several Companies bubble—
>
> As soon as they're floated,
> I'm freely bank-noted—
>   I'm pretty well paid for my trouble.

The duke did well endorsing products he did not use and business ventures to which he lent only his name. Both sources of endorsement income that were available to the duke remain open to the notables of our day, although subjected to increasing scrutiny by the public. In 1971 the Federal Trade Commission had occasion to question whether veterans of the Indianapolis 500 had sufficient expertise in toy cars to justify their endorsements for the Mattel Company. Government inquiries have also considered whether certain franchise systems that invoke the names of heroes of the sports world are actually engaging the time and energies of the great men.

But the Duke of Plaza-Toro is not only aware of the profit to be drawn from business endorsements; he is also the first Gilbert character to evince knowledge of the advantages of incorporation under the Companies Act of 1862. That statute, on which Gilbert was to lavish his satirical attentions, is often regarded as the source of modern English corporation law and has been referred to as the "magna carta of cooperative enterprise." Actually, the act was not an innovative piece of legislation but merely the recodification of a number of earlier nineteenth-century statutory developments. The history of modern company law, to use the British terminology, began in 1825 with the repeal of the Bubble Act, which had been passed in 1720 in reaction to a series of fraudulent securities offerings of which the so-called "South Sea Bubble" was the most famous. Until its repeal in 1825, the Bubble Act generally prohibited the use of corporations unless their formation was specially authorized by act of Parliament or royal charter. By a series of separate acts beginning with 1825, the availability of corporate business forms was gradually expanded, although the privilege of limited liability that is the hallmark of the modern corporation was introduced only by the Joint Stock Companies Act of 1856. The principal function of the Companies Act of 1862 was to consolidate the 1856 act with five statutes subsequently passed and to elaborate the provisions dealing with liquidation ("winding up") of corporations.

In *The Gondoliers* the Duke of Plaza-Toro, although very much a nobleman, is "unhappily in straitened circumstances at present" and sees advantages in incorporation. Feeling that his social influence is much more extensive than his personal resources, he has permitted a syndicate to organize a corporation to exploit him. The company is to be called the Duke of Plaza-Toro, Limited. An influential directorate has been secured by the syndicate, and the duke himself is to join the board after the original shares have been allotted.

Somehow, Gilbert always seemed to associate the prospect of formation of a corporation with the ultimate possibility of liquidation without the full satisfaction of its creditors. The duke's daughter, who has been pronounced Queen of Barataria, expresses concern that she "may be called upon at any time to witness her honoured sire in process of liquidation." The duchess is compelled to acknowledge that possibility but turns

Gilbert reading *Utopia, Limited* to the cast at the Savoy Theatre. To the right of Gilbert are Sullivan and D'Oyly Carte.

aside her daughter's worry with a typical Gilbertian pun: "If your father should stop, it will, of course be necessary to wind him up." Happily, *The Gondoliers* comes to a conclusion before the duke's company has an opportunity to fall on evil days. In fact, we learn in Act 2 that, although the duke personally is ninety-five quarters in arrear, he has just been floated at a premium and registered under the Limited Liability Act. We must, however, remain in doubt as to whether the success of the offering would have changed the first reaction of the duke's daughter that there was something "degrading" in the concept of "a Grandee of Spain turned into a public company."

In *Utopia, Limited,* written four years later, the comic prospect was to broaden into the panorama of an entire society transforming itself into a public corporation under the Companies Act of 1862. The opera tells of a tropical island country, Utopia, that has had great difficulty choosing an appropriate form of government. After unsuccessful experiments in democracy, it has hit on a dangerous variant of the notion of constitutional monarchy. The king of Utopia is trailed around by a bomb-laden official, named the Public Exploder, who is authorized to blow the king up on "his very first lapse from political or social propriety." The governmental form thus evolved is described by a courtier as "a Despotism tempered by Dynamite." (In the twentieth century, we had cause to wonder, in view of the eruption of violence into American political processes, whether our country was not becoming a Republic tempered by Revolvers.)

An opportunity for a further reform of Utopian society is provided by the return of its Princess Zara from England, where she has taken a high academic degree. She brings home with her a delegation consisting of representatives of the main bulwarks of British society whose mission is to remake Utopia in the image of Great Britain. The delegation, named the Flowers of Progress, consists of a British lord chamberlain, officers of the army and navy (including our old friend Captain Corcoran from the good ship *Pinafore*), a queen's counsel and member of Parliament who represents both law and national government, and a spokesman for the new county council system that had just been introduced in England. A leading member of the delegation is Mr. Goldbury, a company promoter. He produces the central idea for the restructuring of Utopia: instead of remaining a monarchy, it should register as a corporation under the Companies Act of 1862. In support of his proposal, he launches into a song in praise of the corporate form, a song that, among its other virtues, contains one of the finest working definitions of corporate capital, at least from the point of view of creditors. Capital, according to Mr. Goldbury, is "a public declaration to what extent they mean to pay their debts." Since Mr. Goldbury's song is a great comic tribute to the corporation and also an important key to Gilbert's corporate satire, it deserves to be set down at length:

> Some seven men form an Association
>   (If possible, all Peers and Baronets),
> They start off with a public declaration
>   To what extent they mean to pay their debts.
> That's called their Capital: if they are wary
>   They will not quote it at a sum immense.
> The figure's immaterial—it may vary
>   From eighteen million down to eighteenpence.
>   *I* should put it rather low;
>   The good sense of doing so
>   Will be evident at once to any debtor.
>   When it's left to you to say
>   What amount you mean to pay,
>   Why, the lower you can put it at, the better.

They then proceed to trade with all who'll trust 'em,
    Quite irrespective of their capital
(It's shady, but it's sanctified by custom);
    Bank, Railway, Loan, or Panama Canal.
You can't embark on trading too tremendous—
    It's strictly fair, and based on common sense—
If you succeed, your profits are stupendous—
    And if you fail, pop goes your eighteenpence.
      Make the money-spinner spin!
      For you only stand to win,
And you'll never with dishonesty be twitted,
      For nobody can know,
      To a million or so,
To what extent your capital's committed!

If you come to grief, and creditors are craving
    (For nothing that is planned by mortal head
Is certain in this Vale of Sorrow—saving
    That one's Liability is Limited),—
Do you suppose that signifies perdition?
    If so you're but a monetary dunce—
You merely file a Winding-Up Petition,
    And start another Company at once!
    Though a Rothschild you may be
    In your own capacity,
As a Company you've come to utter sorrow—
    But the Liquidators say,
    "Never mind—you needn't pay,"
So you start another Company to-morrow!

The gospel of the corporation, as recited by Goldbury, at first sight strikes the king of Utopia as dishonest, but he concludes that if it's good enough for virtuous England, it's good enough for his own backward island. The royal court, given the green light by its monarch's approval, takes up Goldbury's project with enthusiasm and, in fact, Act 1 of *Utopia, Limited* concludes with what may be the only choral tribute to a corporation statute in all the pages of opera:

All hail, astonishing Fact!
  All hail, Invention new—
The Joint Stock Company's Act—
  The Act of Sixty-Two!

The second act shows the far-reaching effects of incorporation on Utopia's economy and political life. Mr. Goldbury, flushed with his success at turning the monarchy into a corporation, carries the reorganization to its logical conclusion. Discarding the theory of the 1862 Act that there is magic in the number seven (the number of individual incorporators required under the act for formation of a corporation), Goldbury has constituted every man, woman, and child in Utopia a limited liability company with liability restricted to the amount of his declared capital. Princess Zara asserts that "there is not a christened baby in Utopia who has not already issued his little Prospectus." The princess's favorite Flower of Progress delegate, Captain Fitzbattleaxe, marvels at the power of a civilization to transmute, by the magic word of incorporation, "a Limited Income into an Income Limited."

Universal incorporation, as Gilbert portrays it, proves more attractive to the promoters than to the corporations' creditors. Scaphio, a judge of Utopia's supreme court, has been moonlighting as an apparel supplier. He contracts to supply the entire nation with a complete set of English clothes (so that they may be Anglicized externally as well as within). When he sends his bills, the customers plead liability limited to a declared capital of eighteen pence and apply to have the debt discharged by corporate liquidation under the winding-up provisions of the Companies Act of 1862. In Gilbert's "corporate state" the king has no jurisdiction over grievances such as Scaphio's but must request him to lay his complaint before the next board meeting of Utopia, Limited.

The device of incorporation also profoundly affects the relations of the king with courtiers (including the disappointed Scaphio) who plot his death. Since the king is no longer a human being but a company, they can no longer blow him up; at best they can only seek to "wind him up" by corporate liquidation proceedings, a small source of emotional satisfaction for the king's violent foes.

Toward the end of the opera, the Flowers of Progress, through their Anglicizing programs, including universal incorporation, have achieved such a stable society that they alienate those who thrive on disorder. The opponents of "progress" then decide to overthrow the works of the reformers by introducing the one overlooked force in English government that will ensure permanent chaos—political parties. With the introduction of party government, the regime of Monarchy, Limited is transformed in a wink into a Limited Monarchy.

Even this brief overview of *Utopia* should provide convincing proof that Darlington is wrong in supposing Gilbert to be ignorant of the nature of corporations. It is of interest, however, to consider why Gilbert found corporations to be a worthy object of satire.

There is no doubt that the "magic" of incorporation particularly appealed to Gilbert's penchant for fantasy. Just as he could never get over the belief that a magic love potion transforming a stern clergyman into an impetuous lover was the most humorous of plot devices, so he found worthy of laughter the legal device that permitted the transformation of individual businessmen into a corporate entity. (How he would have roared with laughter had he learned with us that Howard Hughes, by a legal assignment to the Rosemont Corporation reciting a $10 consideration, could literally transform his life and all biographical rights into a corporate asset!)

But if we pause to focus on Gilbert's view of the corporate idea as a false denial of the uncertainties of human life, we will have come to an understanding of a deeper layer of his criticism of the corporation. Gilbert's most personal view of life, at least as he grew older, appears to have been strongly pessimistic. An ensemble in *Utopia* summarizes the human condition in as dark a color as the final chorus from Verdi's *Falstaff*.

> Ill you've thriven—
>   Ne'er in clover;
> Lastly, when
> Three-score and ten
> (And not till then)
>   The joke is over!

To Gilbert, the corporation and the doctrine of limited liability are symbols of artificial endeavors to insulate the individual from the ever-present possibility of disaster in his affairs. As Mr. Goldbury comments in his song of corporations, "For nothing that is planned by mortal head / Is certain in this Vale of Sorrow—saving / That one's Liability is Limited."

More narrowly, the corporate idea to Gilbert was faulty in that it shielded the incompetent and the irresponsible man from the consequences of his own failure. It is for this reason that Gilbert leapt with special delight on the provisions for discharge of corporate obligations through the liquidation, or winding-up, provisions of the Companies Act of 1862. We can be reasonably sure that he was thinking in this connection not only of the business world at large but also of his own world of the theater. In his short play "Actors, Authors, and Audiences" (1890), he deals with failure of a theater manager in much the same manner as he attacks corporate liquidation in *Utopia:* "[Theatre management] is a very easy profession to master. If you make a success, you pocket the profits; if you fail, you close your theatre abruptly, and a benefit performance is organized on your behalf. Then you begin again." Compare the words of Mr. Goldbury in *Utopia* on the delights of corporate winding-up:

> As a Company you've come to utter sorrow—
> > But the Liquidators say,
> > "Never mind—you needn't pay,"
> So you start another Company to-morrow!

Perhaps Gilbert's identification of corporate problems with theater management had been strengthened by the fact that *Utopia* was written shortly after his famous quarrels with his partners, Sullivan and D'Oyly Carte, over the administration of the Savoy Theatre. The equivalence between corporation and theater survived in the last Gilbert and Sullivan opera, *The Grand Duke* (1896), in which Gilbert unsuccessfully mimicked *Utopia* by describing a conspiracy by a group of actors to overthrow a dukedom and remodel it along the lines of a theatrical company.

The most interesting element of Gilbert's criticism of the corporation, however, lies in his suggestion that the privileges of incorporation, public corporate financing, and limited liability are undeserved unless accompanied by compliance with high standards of responsibility by corporate management. The corporate form for the promoter Goldbury is a device for raising funds from the public for doubtful schemes and with minimal risk of accountability. To the populace of Utopia it becomes a means of buying goods for which it has neither the means nor the intention to pay.

The force of Gilbert's attack on corporate morality appears to have been lost on even perceptive observers. George Bernard Shaw, reviewing *Utopia* as a music critic for London's *Saturday Review,* wrote that he "enjoyed the score of Utopia more than that of any previous Savoy operas" and that "the book has Mr. Gilbert's lighter qualities without his faults." However, he scantly summarized Gilbert's "main idea" as "the Anglicization of Utopia by a people boundlessly credulous as to the superiority of the English race" and made no reference to the satire of principles of corporate law and practice. *Punch,* unlike Shaw, was extremely critical of *Utopia.* Its 1893 review of the new offering of the team that the magazine had taken to calling "Gillivan and Sulbert" (in tribute, one would hope, to the uncanny blending of their gifts) made no substantial comment on the book except to accuse Gilbert of plagiarizing a scene presenting a court reception in the semicircular stage arrangement popularized by the Christy Minstrels.

Even with the advantage of historical retrospection, twentieth-century critics often failed to see that the corporate law satire was firmly rooted in the business scandals in Gilbert's times. Thus W. A. Darlington writes of *Utopia:* "It would be interesting to know just why Gilbert fell foul of the Joint Stock Company Act of 1862 at this particular period in his life, more than a quarter of a century after the act had become law." Clues to the answer to Darlington's question are provided for all to see in Mr. Goldbury's song, in which he sings of the management of the spanking-new, thinly incorporated firm:

> They then proceed to trade with all who'll trust 'em,
> Quite irrespective of their capital
> (It's shady, but it's sanctified by custom);
> Bank, Railway, Loan, or Panama Canal.

These lines reveal that Gilbert was not merely attacking the concept of limited liability as an abstraction, but that he was well aware of frauds that had been perpetrated on the public by unprincipled men using the advantages of corporate form.

The reference to banks in Mr. Goldbury's song might have awakened memories of a number of bank failures in England in the latter part of the nineteenth century, but it is likely that Gilbert intended to allude to the Glasgow Bank fraud case of 1878. The closing of the City of Glasgow Bank in October 1878 led to criminal proceedings resulting in the conviction of five directors and the bank manager on charges relating to the falsification of balance sheets. It was asserted that the directors had produced false balance sheets and declared large dividends in order to cover up the insolvency of the bank. The bank's downfall had been contributed to by improvident loans, including those extended lavishly to the defendant directors and their firms.

The City of Glasgow Bank had lost no time in incorporating under the Joint Stock Company Act of 1862 in the very year of its adoption, and Gilbert may be forgiven for doubting whether the insiders had in their stewardship justified the protection given to them by the new legislation. Arthur Griffiths's account of the behavior of one of the directors prior to the bank's closing could hardly have been bettered by Gilbert's own pen: "One shareholder in September, a month before the failure, called at the office of Mr. Stewart, saying he had heard unpleasant rumours about the bank. Mr. Stewart, a director, who . . . was largely in debt to the bank, answered that there were always rumours current about everybody. Then Mr. Stewart went out and did not return, being clearly anxious to cut short an inconvenient interview."

The most recent business scandal referred to in the quoted lines of Mr. Goldbury's song was the welter of criminal charges growing out of the failure of the Panama Canal construction program undertaken by the French-controlled Panama Company. In February 1893, eight months prior to the opening of *Utopia,* the aged Ferdinand de Lesseps, hero of the building of the Suez Canal, and his son and two other men were found guilty of fraud in an 1888 bond issue to raise funds for the canal project, of attempted fraud in another aborted bond issue, and of misappropriation of company funds. The fraud charges—expressed in the elegant language of French statute as the use of fraudulent means to raise hopes for the realization of a chimerical event—rested on misrepresentations made by the defendants with respect to the cost and likely completion date of the canal and levels of expected revenues. Although the conviction was upset on appeal (on the basis of the statute of limitations) before *Utopia* opened, the facts of the case lingered.

In March of the same year, five French legislators, the former public works minister and his private secretary, and the younger de Lesseps faced a bribery trial in which it was alleged that the public officials had been bribed by the Panama Company in an effort to secure favorable legislation and governmental action in connection with the company's financing plans. The legislators were acquitted, but the other defendants were found guilty.

The accusations of misconduct, which were the subject of these trials, only singled out from a bizarre pattern of financial behavior those acts with which the criminal law of the time could most easily come to grips. Very little of the procedure used in the Panama Canal financings bears any resemblance to what might be considered permissible under the regulatory system of our own Securities and Exchange Commission. In addition to their attempts on the integrity of the French government, the administrators of the Canal Company made widespread use of company funds to pay newspapers for publishing favorable stories on the progress of the canal. Far from considering such payments to reflect doubtful business morality, the Canal Company reported such payments in its financial statements under the wonderfully euphemistic account heading *publicité*. Apparently the newspapermen were even less shy about the payments than the company and considered the amount of the payoffs to afford a measure of the value of their editorial pages. Maron J. Simon reports in his study of the canal scandals that one editor sued the auditor for the liquidated company for understating the amounts that the Panama Company had paid his newspaper.

The events in France were not lost on Gilbert or on the English public. The *Times of London* carried detailed stories on the Panama enterprise and the litigation that resulted. Moreover, by the spring of 1893 much of the passion and curiosity aroused by the Panama affair had focused on the figure of a "mystery man" then residing in England—Cornelius Herz, an international charlatan, confidence man, and friend of influential men in political and financial circles. Herz, who had been accused of complicity in the Panama scandal, was, during the whole of 1893 and for many years thereafter, holed up in the Tankerville Hotel in Bournemouth, England, where he waged a successful battle against extradition to France on the basis of his medical condition. The French legislators, in their eagerness to talk to Herz, resolved that if illness would not permit him to come to them, they would question him at his bedside. However, the interview, which was scheduled for July 1897, never came off. Herz reneged at the last minute, and this disappointing news was transmitted to the group of twenty-five deputies just as they were about to board the Channel steamer.

Although the Panama Canal case continued to make history for many years, by 1893 it had already been assured a measure of immortality in the words and music of *Utopia, Limited*. It was an affair that supplied all the major elements of Gilbert's satirical view of corporate finance—the famous man whose name inspired investors' confidence (de Lesseps); a securities offering based on unjustified claims of bonanza; the "free bank-noting" of newspapers and others whose sponsorship of the offering was desired; and finally the liquidation of failed corporate enterprise. Despite his jokes at the expense of the corporation and limited liability, and his likely disillusionment with the business practices of his own time, Gilbert shows such balanced judgment in his works that we cannot assume he was proposing an outright repeal of the Companies Act of 1862. Indeed, if he attacked limited liability in *Utopia,* we must recall that in the earlier *Pirates of Penzance* (1879) he assaulted with equal force the notion of unlimited individual liability, the observance of contract unmodified by protective considerations of public policy. In that opera the young hero, Frederic, is mocked by Gilbert as a "slave of duty" because he undertakes literal and strict performance of his pirate apprenticeship until his twenty-first birthday as provided by his indenture, even though the term of performance will last eighty-four years since his birthday falls on February 29.

In fact, I am not sure that Gilbert's critique of the corporation is inapposite to the debate that continues in modern governmental and academic circles as to the proper scope of corporate responsibilities. In return for the protections and privileges of corporate form and the opportunities of large business corporations to amass wealth and power, the expectations for social contribution by corporations have greatly increased. Discussions that decades ago turned on obligations of corporations for charitable gifts and local community activity have broadened to include demands relating to basic business policy, such as ecological and safety concerns, minority-group hiring, and corporate attitudes toward war and colonialism. Nobody would hazard a guess where Gilbert would have stood on the myriad of public issues faced by the modern corporation, but I think he would have been at home with the notion that the responsibility of a corporation may be far broader than its legal liability.

It is difficult to come away from a study of *Utopia, Limited* and of Gilbert's other literary expressions of interest in law and crime without feeling that his work has suffered the double injustice of having been denied "relevancy" either to the problems of posterity or to the important issues of his own day. How much better we would do were we to read his librettos in the spirit of the counsel given by the jester, Jack Point, in *The Yeomen of the Guard:*

Oh, winnow all my folly, and you'll find
A grain or two of truth among the chaff!

Bibliographical Notes

Biographical and critical sources quoted in the article are from Leslie Baily, *The Gilbert and Sullivan Book* (London: Cassell, 1952), 212, 213, 400; W. A. Darlington, *The World of Gilbert and Sullivan* (New York: Crowell, 1950), 173–74; and Hesketh Pearson, *Gilbert, His Life and Strife* (New York: Harper, 1957), 19, 83, 264–65.

The quotations from *Thespis, The Pirates of Penzance, Iolanthe, The Yeomen of the Guard, The Gondoliers,* and *Utopia, Limited* are drawn from *Plays and Poems of W. S. Gilbert,* preface by Deems Taylor (New York: Random House, 1932). Quotations from Gilbert's short stories and articles, "My Maiden Brief," "Actors, Authors, and Audiences," and "The Wicked World" appear in W. S. Gilbert, *Foggerty's Fairy and Other Tales* (London, 1890). Gilbert's short play on capital punishment, "The Hooligan," is included in his *Original Plays: Fourth Series* (London: Chatto and Windus, 1922).

For the history of the Companies Act of 1862, see Clive M. Schmitthoff and James H. Thompson, eds., *Palmer's Company Law,* 21st ed. (London: Stevens, 1968), 5–9; William Holdsworth, *A History of English Law,* vol. 15 (London: Methuen, 1965), 49–59.

Shaw's review of *Utopia* is found in Eric Bentley, ed., *Shaw on Music: A Selection from the Music Criticism of Bernard Shaw* (Garden City, N.Y.: Doubleday, 1955), 216, 219. For *Punch*'s review, see *Punch* 105 (Oct. 28, 1893): 204. Despite its critical rejection of the opera, there is evidence that Gilbert's corporate satire became a part of the magazine's comic worldview. A cartoon published three years later depicts a proposed financing of the Ottoman Empire by the Western powers. The Ottoman Empire is shown being reorganized as a corporation under the name "Turkey, Limited" (*Punch* 111 [Nov. 28, 1896]: 259).

For a report of the Glasgow Bank trial, see William Wallace, ed., *Trial of the City of Glasgow Bank Directors* (Glasgow: William Hodge, 1905) in the Notable Scottish Trials series. See also Arthur Griffiths, *Mysteries of Police and Crime,* vol. 2 (London: Cassell, 1899), 390.

An account of the Panama Canal scandal can be found in Maron J. Simon, *The Panama Affair* (New York: Scribner, 1971). Many of the facts relating to the Panama case to which I make reference are drawn from Simon's interesting book. For an eyewitness report of the Panama trials, see Albert Bataille, *Causes Criminelles et Mondaines de 1893* (Paris: Dentu, 1894), 1–314.

Aspects of law in Gilbert and Sullivan operas are discussed in Andrew Goodman, *Gilbert and Sullivan at Law* (East Brunswick, N.J.: Fairleigh Dickinson Univ. Press, 1983), citing the present article as "most informative in this area," 225.

11

"Pore Jud is Daid": Violence and Lawlessness in the Plays of Lynn Riggs

Ben Brantley, drama critic of the *New York Times,* has credited Trevor Nunn's 1998 production of *Oklahoma!* with letting us see more clearly the shadows that have always been cast by the "bright golden haze on the meadow." The interplay between the light and the dark, between exuberant optimism and the threat of violence, lies at the very heart of the Rodgers and Hammerstein musical and of the "folk-play" from which it was faithfully adapted, Lynn Riggs's *Green Grow the Lilacs.* After the New York opening of *Oklahoma!* in 1943, Hammerstein publicly acknowledged the heavy debt that he owed to Riggs's original stage work: "I should like to go on record as saying that Mr. Riggs's play is the wellspring of almost all that is good in *Oklahoma!* I kept many of the lines of the original play without making any changes in them at all for the simple reason that they could not be improved on. . . . Lynn Riggs and *Green Grow the Lilacs* are the very soul of *Oklahoma!"* Among the Riggs inventions preserved in *Oklahoma!*'s book and lyrics, though often overlooked by audiences enthralled by Richard Rodgers's melodious score, is an uncannily prescient delineation of a serial killer. In *Green Grow the Lilacs* the homicidal farmhand who menaces the peace of a rural community near Tulsa in the Indian Territory during the summer of 1900 is named Jeeter Fry; ever mindful of singability, Hammerstein changed the villain's first name to Jud. Fry seems to be the supreme embodiment of what Riggs sensed as a potential for evil and calamity that secretly imperiled Oklahoma life during his childhood. Riggs wrote of this feeling of unease: "When I was a child there, the country and the people were very dramatic. A primitive violence was always close to the surface, always apt to break out at any moment. It was all about me. Under a sometimes casual exterior, there was a fever and a thrumming. Just by accident of nerves, I suppose, I was always conscious of this hidden excitement." The sources of this "hidden excitement," an emotion that persisted through Riggs's formative years, may have included the lawless environment of early Oklahoma, a tragic outbreak of racial violence in the region where Riggs grew to manhood, and disasters in his family history.

A Child of Oklahoma's Outlaw Era

Rollie Lynn Riggs was born on August 31, 1899, on a farm three miles southwest of Claremore in the Tulsa area of the Indian Territory. His father, William, was a rancher at the time of his son's birth and later became president of a Claremore bank. Lynn's mother, Rosie, was one-eighth Cherokee and accordingly entitled to an allotment of 160 acres of land under the Dawes Act of 1887; after her death of typhoid fever in 1901, baby Lynn received a portion of her land under his father's guardianship. In 1902 Bill Riggs married Juliette Chambers, one-fourth Cherokee, who proved cold to his children and served as the prototype of the harsh, cruel stepmothers who appear in Riggs's work. When Juliette's anger would boil over, Bill Riggs sent the children to stay with his sister, Mary Riggs Thompson, who provided Lynn "some of the mothering he lacked at home"; Aunt Mary became the loving and wise Aunt Eller of *Green Grow the Lilacs*.

Succeeding generations remember Lynn Riggs as poet, Southwestern regional dramatist, and writer of scripts for such Hollywood films as *The Plainsman,* starring Gary Cooper, and the Marlene Dietrich vehicle *The Garden of Allah*. His early years, however, provided him a generous sampling of ranching and white-collar experience that helped him develop the realist vein that came to predominate in his writing. In 1928 Riggs summarized his life to date in a deprecating postscript when he answered a letter from Barrett H. Clark, of drama publisher and agency Samuel French, Inc., requesting an autobiography: "Would you rather know that I've farmed, punched cattle, been night clerk in a small Oklahoma hotel, ridden a freight to Chicago, worked for an express company, played extra in dozens of movies, clerked in Macy's, read proof for various newspapers, reported, sung all over the middle west one summer in chautauqua, taught English, published poems, worked on a ranch, etc."

The great range of Riggs's occupations, many of which would be familiar to young Americans trying their hands at entry-level jobs, should not disguise the fact that he was born into and remained under the spell of Oklahoma's outlaw era. In 1892, only seven years before Riggs's birth, the Daltons, after strengthening their gang in Oklahoma, were shot to pieces during a vainglorious robbery of two banks in broad daylight at Coffeyville, Kansas. Dalton gang member Bill Doolin luckily dropped out of the raiding party at the last moment, claiming that his horse had gone lame and that he had to steal a replacement. After the Coffeyville disaster, Doolin organized a new band of desperadoes, the Oklahombres, whom the outlaw's nemesis, U.S. Marshal Evett Dumas Nix called "the most vicious outlaw gang the Southwest ever was to know." The Oklahombres eluded a large posse in 1893 after waging a celebrated gunfight at Ingalls, Oklahoma. According to the orthodox version of Doolin lore, Deputy Marshal Heck Thomas shot the outlaw leader to death in 1896 on a dusty road near his hideout in the area of Lawton, Oklahoma.

Tulsa police historian Ronald L. Trekell notes that although the Doolin gang "never plundered or killed in Tulsa, they passed through often." For Tulsans, and Oklahomans in general, the Doolins enjoy a heroic stature comparable to the preeminence of the James gang in Missouri. Even Marshal Nix, if we are to trust the words of his ghostwriter, Gordon Hines, was lavish in praise of his old adversary, Bill Doolin: "I don't believe Bill Doolin ever shot a victim in the back and I know very well he didn't make a practice of robbing needy individuals of their petty all. He and his gang went after organized capital—the railroads, banks and express companies. If he took a horse or forced a lonely rancher to feed his men, it was because of dire necessity and he always tried to compensate the person who was called upon for help."

Other outlaws flourishing in the last days of the Indian Territory included the part-Cherokee Crawford Goldsby ("Cherokee Bill"), who reputedly killed thirteen victims before his twentieth birthday; and a gang led by a Euchee Indian named Rufus Buck that went on a "ten-day spree of rape, robbery and murder" in 1895. Many of Oklahoma's desperadoes continued their outrages during Lynn Riggs's lifetime. The killings by the Bert Casey gang ended only in 1902 when Casey and Jim Sims were shot by special deputies in Cleo Springs. By the standards of his generation, part-Cherokee bank robber and murderer Henry Starr was a champion of criminal longevity; born in 1873, he died of wounds suffered at a failed Arkansas bank robbery in 1921.

The white and Indian outlaws of Oklahoma, transformed by poetic vision, reappear in many of the plays of Lynn Riggs. Sometimes they become comic or heroic figures of frontier myth that symbolize a yearning for freedom from social constraint. At other times, however, the career or habitual criminal is stripped of glamour and embodies the menace and destructive impulse that Riggs felt stirring beneath the soil of his native state.

The 1920 Claremore Fire and the 1928 Sapulpa Shooting

Riggs's acute sensitivity to disaster likened the ravages of nature to mankind's cruelty. In *Russet Mantle,* produced on Broadway in 1936, the poet Galt makes this analogy explicit.

> Here we are in a land, vast and beautiful and fertile. Seeds in the earth push up. They blossom, they feed us. Sometimes there's no rain—last summer there wasn't—and the soil that ought to bear becomes instead a blowing and drifting terror. . . . The papers call it a drought. Sometimes there are cloudbursts—you have them out here. . . . Sometimes a winter when sleet and snow and wind are slashing and venomous. But what happens? The cold stops. Rains fall. The sun shines. The rigors and terrors of Nature come to an end. *But the rigor and terror of man against man never cease.* I've seen it. I know! In textile mills, railroad yards, on docks, in the streets. Machine guns mowing down men in Wisconsin. Men and women hounded and flogged and tortured in San Francisco. Riot squads, strike breakers, nausea gas—bayonets! And starvation.

Nature's threats constantly loomed over Riggs's Oklahoma. Tulsa lies in a tornado alley. The city maintains a siren system to warn of oncoming storm or flood. Although the metropolis had long been spared, a monstrous twister descended nearby in May 1999, causing heavy damage to the Oklahoma City suburbs and the town of Stroud on the turnpike leading to the city. Another danger is posed to Oklahomans in the spring by prairie fires whipped by dry March winds, a far cry from the sweet wind that "comes right behind the rain" in the pages of the Rodgers and Hammerstein anthem.

The fear of fire, whether of natural origin or due to human agency, is a pervasive theme of *Green Grow the Lilacs*. On inquiry among the playwright's surviving relatives, I have encountered a recollection that Riggs, about eight years before the play's composition, had a close brush with a fire of unexplained cause at the home of his beloved aunt, Mary Riggs Thompson. After her second marriage, to John Brice, Aunt Mary had given up the management of a boardinghouse adjoining the St. James Hotel in Claremore and moved to a farmhouse west of the town near the road to Collinsville. About 1920, during the Christmas season, Lynn Riggs paid a visit to Aunt Mary; others staying at the house were his first cousin Willie Thompson (the original Ado Annie), his eight-year-old first cousin (once removed) Howard McNeill (whose mother, Laura, inspired the character of Laurey), and Howard's three-year-old sister, Mary Jane. As Mr. McNeill, now deceased, recalled in a 2002 telephone conversation with me, when he was over ninety, "Uncle" Lynn left for the Claremore train station around midnight on Christmas Eve. In the course of the night a fire broke out. A wall of the farmhouse collapsed in flames; the family's dogs barked, alerting the household. Howard escaped and was relieved to see his grandmother carry little Mary Jane to safety. To the day Howard spoke with me, he could not account for the fire but noted that both Lynn and Aunt Willie were smokers.

It is tempting to speculate whether the Claremore fire may have remained in Lynn Riggs's mind when he brought *Green Grow the Lilacs* to its climax with the attempted torching of the Williams farm before the horrified eyes of Laurey and Aunt Eller. There is no doubt, however, that a violent family tragedy in Sapulpa, Oklahoma, dating from 1928, the year before *Green Grow the Lilacs* was written, haunted the dramatist during the rest of his life.

On Easter Sunday, April 8, 1928, Bessie Thompson was arrested in the fatal shooting at two o'clock that morning of her husband, Raymond, Riggs's first cousin. Raymond was "shot twice through the left side, one bullet going through his arm also. He lived a few minutes after he was shot, but was unable to speak." The tragedy occurred at a rooming house called the Midway Rooms, where the Thompson couple resided; the establishment was operated by Ray's sister, Dollie (Mrs. Arthur R. Woods). Dollie told the police that Bessie "turned the gun on herself as she entered [the Thompsons'] room, shooting twice through her left breast"; doctors found only superficial flesh wounds. The arresting officers found Bessie in a bloody night dress standing over her husband. When a physician told her that he was dying, she bent down to Ray for a last kiss. Her request to attend his funeral was denied, but she was permitted to help relatives select a casket.

Raymond, age forty-two, was nine years younger than Bessie; they had no children. He had been employed by the Frisco (St. Louis & San Francisco) Railroad until eye trouble forced him to change jobs. At her trial the following month, Bessie testified, in the support of her defenses of self-defense and temporary insanity, that she was afraid that Ray, to whom she had been wed sixteen years before, would kill her. At a party they attended on the evening before the shooting, Ray had danced with a young woman, Bessie calmly told the jury with an occasional tear; he had then attempted unsuccessfully to leave the party without his encumbering wife. After they reached home, he cursed Bessie as a spoilsport, grabbed and bruised her, and locked her out of their bedroom. When she broke the latch, he went for a .38 caliber revolver lying in the tray of a trunk, but she seized it first and fired twice. She then turned the gun on herself. She had only a "hazy memory" of what happened afterward.

On May 23, after a brief nocturnal deliberation, the jury acquitted Bessie Thompson, setting her free only about a month and a half after the homicide. The county court seemed to show great tenderness for criminal defendants that year. In its issue of May 24, 1928, the *Sapulpa Herald* set the Thompson acquittal in context: "This case was the last one tried on the criminal term of court which opened here May 15. Only two convictions were returned during the term. In both cases, the charge was burglary."

Raymond Thompson's sixteen-year-old nephew, Howard McNeill, who had witnessed the Claremore fire, was staying at his Aunt Dollie's rooming house on the fatal Easter morning. He had never seen a corpse before, and he never forgot the horrifying image of Raymond's staring eyes. Unsurprisingly, McNeill and his relatives do not concur with the jury's speedy verdict. According to McNeill, Ray's sisters never much cared for their sister-in-law Bessie, whom they regarded as "domineering." The Thompsons believed that Bessie had shot her husband because he was planning to leave her. Family loyalties became entangled in the aftermath of the shooting, because Charley Warner, the husband of Ray's sister Lillie, was Bessie's nephew. McNeill recalls that arguments over the trial brought the Warners to the brink of divorce.

From March 1953 until shortly before his death of cancer in June 1954, Lynn Riggs was working intensively on the adaptation of the Sapulpa murder case in a novel to be entitled "The Affair at Easter." His plans for the book, of which three of five projected parts were completed, signaled an intention to universalize the significance of his family's tragedy by sounding his often reiterated theme of ever-present human cruelties patterned on the harshness of nature. The very first words of the typescript, as it has been left to us, starkly announce, "Loose in the world is a floating malice." A preliminary entry in his working notebook raises the possibility of concluding each of the novel's sections—"Easter Morning," "Georgia's My Home," "Hide Me from Heaven," "Summer Solstice," and "Truth to Tell"—with actual or impending violence. In the epigraphs of the novel's sections, Riggs preannounces an analogy between human brutality and nature's rages by adopting successive phrases drawn from the only surviving stanza of an unfinished poem by Gerard Manley Hopkins:

Strike, churl; hurl, cheerless wind, then; heltering hail
May's beauty massacre and wispèd wild clouds grow
Out on the giant air; tell Summer No,
Bid joy back, have at the harvest, keep Hope pale.

Structuring his novel (possibly as an "allegory" or "parable") within this scheme of universal unease, Riggs at the same time followed his customary bent for identifying his characters and settings with people and places he knew well. On March 14, 1953, the first day of entries in his working notebook, he addressed the need to "get the names settled" and to "get the characters straight at once." The principal figures in the novel and their real-life equivalents included:

Fictional character	Based on
Della (Jonson) Hogan, proprietor of Royal Hotel, Siloam, first wife of Wade Hogan	Margie May "Dollie" Thompson (Mrs. Art Woods), operator of Midway Rooms, Sapulpa
Marnen Glory Hogan, Della's sister, second wife of Wade Hogan	Willie Roberta Thompson, married to Art Woods about 1935 after the death of her sister Dollie; Willie Thompson inspired Ado Annie in *Green Grow the Lilacs*
Rod Jonson, husband and shooting victim of his wife, Beth; brother of Della and Marnen Glory	Ray Thompson, shot by his wife, Bessie, in Sapulpa in 1928

Fictional character	Based on
Beth Jonson	Bessie Thompson
Wade Hogan	Art Woods
Caleb White, "stepfather" of the Jonson siblings but perhaps bigamously married to their mother, Emma, deceased	A man identified by Riggs only as John B., probably John Brice, Mary Riggs Thompson's second husband; like White, Brice was an itinerant worker

The author's personal resemblances to certain of the novel's characters grew more complex as his plotting developed. The second entry in his working notebook suggested that Beth's recital of her version of the shooting might be made "to me—or someone like me—in the cell." In the initial table of characters, the role of the prisoner's confidant is Rod Jonson's cousin, Professor Andrew Tabor. Andy's identification with Lynn Riggs is confirmed in the table of the characters' real-life correspondences where Riggs's name is abbreviated by the initials R.L. (i.e., Rollie Lynn, the author's first names). The same initials also identify the playwright as the source for the professor's son, the college student Brad Tabor, who was to play a crucial role in the novel's plot.

Riggs's initial idea, which he compared to that of the celebrated 1950 Japanese film *Rashomon,* was to have different people telling the major story of the "killing of Ray" but in doing so to "tell richly . . . character and a time." To all appearances, he was more successful in creating characters than in evoking the period of the action: although Riggs alternatively considered setting the novel's principal events either in 1940, twelve years after the Sapulpa murder, or in the present, 1953, he did not create a social ambience that is sufficiently detailed to reflect convincingly the era of World War II or its aftermath.

In the three completed sections of his novel, Riggs adhered to his plan of utilizing multiple points of view, but the extensive use of flashbacks sometimes weakens the focus on varying interpretations of the Easter shooting. As the story begins, Beth Jonson, who has been convicted of Rod's murder, writes to Andy Tabor complaining of the family's false testimony, asking him to hear her side of the story and asserting that the shooting was accidental or, at worst, in self-defense. In a postscript Beth darkly hints, "Besides—you're more tied up in this thing than maybe you know. I wouldn't want to do anything about that, though. Nuff Sed." The direction of the implied threat will eventually be made plain, but the post-script immediately shows one of the main reasons that, even apart from the killing, the Jonson family detests Beth: she is an inveterate snoop and eavesdropper who is often right about her in-laws' conduct but consistently misreads their motives. As the novel proceeds, Riggs reveals many crimes and scandals within the Jonson family that richly merited Beth's prying: Caleb White's possible guilt of bigamy and murder; the operation of a bootlegging and gambling joint by Wade Hogan and his second wife, Marnen Glory; the irresponsible Marnen Glory's conception of her daughter Inez with Wade while he was still married to Della; Inez's brutal deflowering by her parents' poker dealer and her affair with Suggs Aker, a married country ballad singer modeled on Gene Autry.

Part One is given over mostly to a narrative, told mainly from Beth's point of view, of the events on Easter morning that culminate in the fatal shooting. The underlying cause of the killing is the years-long marital discord between Rod and the chronically unfaithful Beth. A bitter quarrel is sparked by Rod's discovering in Room 2 of the hotel a green tie with polka dots that he had given to his Uncle Walt, with whom Beth has been having an affair; Beth spent the previous night with her lover, who had registered at the Royal Hotel under a fictitious name. (In her reveries she refers to him only as "Mr. Big and Beautiful.") As the spouses' angry words intensify, he caps the quarrel by taunting her, "I don't even care if you laid up with your own daddy—which I have no doubt you did, from the age of ten on!" She hurls a heavy hairbrush at him; she calls his deceased mother, Emma, not much better than a "very ordinary whore" for marrying Caleb White while his first wife was still alive. Rod goes for a gun and is shot as Beth struggles to wrest it away. As he flees down the rickety backstairs of the hotel and she stands on the platform above, the "gun she had been clutching all this time suddenly exploded with a horrible sound right in her hand." She passes out as her mortally wounded husband falls into the bushes below.

At the beginning of Part Two ("Georgia's My Home"), which recounts the immediate aftermath of the killing, Della proves herself to be Beth's deadliest antagonist. Ranting that "hangin's too good" for her, she presses Caleb White to give false testimony against her sister-in-law. She reminds her stepfather that he is a fugitive from justice because, as her mother had told her, he had slain his first spouse's lover, Blaise Hyatt, in North Carolina. In the long flashback that follows, it turns out that Caleb killed

his rival in self-defense, but Della has adeptly played on his fear of prosecution and on his irrational belief that stern justice for Beth's crime will
compensate for his own escape from the law.

In Part Three of "The Affair at Easter" ("Hide Me from Heaven"), Della
plays another trick to support her assertion that she had seen Beth fire the
second bullet after taking careful aim. In fact, Della had not observed the
fatal shot. After Rod's death, however, she scraped away a patch of the black
paint that covered the surface of a window in her hotel room; only by means
of this covert alteration was the backstairs platform rendered visible from
Della's room, where she had claimed to be at the time of the shooting.

Only a little more than two pages of projected Part Four ("Summer
Solstice") were written, but they are sufficient to disclose the secret to
which Beth alluded in her letter to Andy Tabor that begins the book. The
small fragment of "Summer Solstice" recalls, from Brad Tabor's point of
view, the beginning of his homosexual passion for Jere Sayville, the young
desk clerk of the Royal Hotel whom Brad meets at Rod Jonson's funeral.
Riggs's working notebook indicates that Jere is in the clutches of a wealthy
and possibly corrupt married couple, the Carters, but that he is trying to
put his life in order. The theme of homosexuality, previously signaled in
Riggs's notes, took on increasing autobiographical significance as drafts
of the novel progressed. In a handwritten reminder on a leaf of his person-
alized memorandum paper, Riggs elaborated his personal identification
with certain of the characters. *Moi* (me), he wrote, boldly underlined, at
the head of the sheet and then listed

Rod (in the branch) [a stream on Uncle Walt's farm that figures in a
    happy childhood scene recalled by Rod Jonson in a dream before
    he wakes to be killed]
Brad & Jere (interchangeably)
Caleb (as young, as old)
Andy.

Riggs's recognition of two homosexual lovers as his "interchangeable" alter egos is remarkable given the reticence he showed about his personal
life. According to Riggs's plans, Andy Tabor was to learn of his son's sexual attachment and to respond with love and understanding.

The concluding Part Five ("Truth to Tell") remains largely a matter for
speculation. Riggs's notes indicate that the section would focus on the in-

terviews Andy Tabor conducted with the Jonson family in an effort to determine the facts of the Easter killing, an investigation that would result in his having greater knowledge of the case than any of the witnesses. In the final scene he would visit Beth in prison and, despite his doubts about the fairness of the trial, would decide to keep silent, after agonizing over the possibility that this course had been influenced by a desire to protect his son and himself. This finale, apparently elaborated from an earlier version of the prison scene intended to be included in Part One, was explained by Riggs in handwritten notes: "Even if they [the witnesses] felt like exerting themselves for Beth, what could they establish? It could only come to their opinion, their guess actually against the firm Gibraltar of Della's statement of what she had seen." Andy's last words, as Riggs left them to us, also favor inaction: " . . . let him be silent. 'God is often so,' he assured himself. If in his own experience, it had fallen to him to watch himself acting in such an exalted capacity, he believed quite genuinely, at last it was not for himself only. It was for them, all those who had been involved. Surely he owed them that much comprehension, that much, in an abstract way, love. Even himself."

The Tulsa Race Riot of 1921

Lynn Riggs's homeland has been bloodied by tribal and racial conflict in the last two centuries. His native town is situated six miles southeast of a twenty-five-acre mound settled by Osage Indians in 1802 at the encouragement of Major Jean-Pierre Chouteau, founder of St. Louis and Kansas City. The mound was named by the French "fair mountain," or "Clermont" (later misspelled "Claremore"). After the Cherokees, displaced from the east, were given title to lands including Claremore Mound, they attempted for years to drive the Osages away, and they succeeded only too well. "Claremore's Historical Summary" recalls the destruction of the Osage community in the so-called Claremore Mound Massacre: "In October 1817, a well-armed band of Cherokee and Delaware Indians attacked the Clermont village. The Osage warriors were away on a hunting trip. The village was filled with women, children and old men. During the attack, many of the Osage Indians got as far as the river, but drowned in an attempt to escape. The others were killed and some taken as prisoners. Chief Clermont [the Osage leader] was killed and buried on the mound."

Antagonisms between whites and blacks of Oklahoma have also erupted with tragic results. Arrell Morgan Gibson, in his history of the state, has

noted that "a Negro-white outbreak . . . occurred in Guthrie during terri-
torial days." This early conflict has been eclipsed by the Tulsa Race Riot of
1921, whose horrors have only been fully recognized in recent years. The
violent confrontation of Tulsa's black and white communities, one of the
deadliest racial clashes in American history, was sparked by a minor incident. On May 30, 1921, an African American shoeshine boy, Dick Rowland, had, probably by accident, fallen against a white female acquaintance, seventeen-year-old Sarah Page, who was operating an elevator in
downtown Tulsa's Drexel Building. After Sarah claimed that she had been
assaulted, Rowland was jailed, and the headline of the *Tulsa Tribune* pre-
dicted that a mob would "lynch Negro tonight." Shooting broke out between white and black mobs around the courthouse where Rowland was
detained in a well-guarded cell and spread through the downtown area.
Early on the following morning, a white army invaded the black Greenwood neighborhood, whose prosperous business district was known as
"the Negro Wall Street." Supported by strafing civil aircraft, the invaders
put Greenwood to the torch and murdered and looted as they advanced.
It is estimated that up to 300 Tulsans lost their lives on both sides of the
racial divide, and thirty-four square blocks of Greenwood were reduced
to rubble. This shameful massacre fell out of the consciousness of most
Oklahomans until the 1971 publication of a fearless exposé by reporter Ed
Wheeler. In February 2001 the Oklahoma Commission to Study the Tulsa
Race Riots of 1921 delivered its report recommending that reparations
be paid to survivors and their descendants. Four months later, Governor
Frank Keating signed into law the Tulsa Race Riot Reconciliation Act establishing a memorial and providing scholarships favoring descendants
of 1921 Greenwood residents.

Although Lynn Riggs did not explicitly address the Tulsa race riot in his
literary works, it is a fair assumption that he had a deep aversion to the
persecution of minorities. Riggs's nephew, Leo Cundiff, now deceased, believed that, because of his Cherokee origin, his uncle sympathized with minority groups, including African Americans. His plays often present with
disapproval the mistreatment accorded disfavored minorities, including a
German American groundlessly suspected of sabotage during World War
II; a Portuguese woman who fears her testimony would not be believed;
Mayans despised by descendants of conquistadores in Mexico; a Mexican
hazed in an American military school; and a Syrian peddler who an Okla-
homan widow fears might beat her daughter daily if he married her.

Two of Riggs's portrayals of racist hatred directed against blacks appear to conjure ghosts of the Tulsa riot. The cast of characters in *Hang on to Love* includes Jasper, who, like Dick Rowland, is an African American boot-black. A gambler and small-town bully, Charley Troglin, "didn't seem to like the way Jasper shined his shoes" and "knocked him clean through the window." When Troglin saunters into the domino parlor, where Dr. Beeman is treating Jasper's injuries, he asks the proprietor Jude Summers what is going on. Jude responds coolly, "Doc Beeman is fixing up a negro somebody forgot was human." The brutal Troglin can think of only one possible explanation for such colorblind sympathy: "From the north, ain't you?" Later in the first act, Jude calls on a memory "deep inside himself": "You've never seen a man hanged, have you? You've never seen him jerking against the wall away up there, and *kicking,* have you? And they let him down and put him in a basket and take him away." Thomas Erhard has argued that this passage "reflects Riggs's horror at the old-time lynchings"; this was a fate that Dick Rowland was spared only because of the vigilance of Sheriff William McCullough, one of the few heroes among the Tulsa authorities.

Riggs revisits the theme of African Americans' marginalization in one of his major plays, *The Cherokee Night* (1930). In Scene 4, set in 1906 in the woods near Claremore, three boys of mixed Cherokee and Anglo blood come upon the traces of a murder among four card-playing black men. Art, one of the youths, speaks contemptuously of blacks and of an earlier occasion when they were expelled from Claremore: "Niggers is funny. They got a funny way. When the niggers was run out of Claremore, Pap said a funny thing. When a nigger would git shot, he wouldn't know it. He'd keep on runnin'." In precisely such a self-congratulatory spirit, Greenwood's invaders bragged of their exploits after the infamous burning of 1921. Leo Cundiff remembered that years after the riot an "old boy" came into the Tulsa-area bank where Leo served as a teller and boasted that he had machine-gunned black people along the railroad track, driving them toward Muskogee.

In his earliest attempt at writing full-length drama, *Big Lake,* written in 1925 and produced by the American Laboratory Theatre two years later with a cast including Stella Adler as Elly, Lynn Riggs established what were to become recurrent features of his stage works: insistence on setting the staged events with great precision in time and community as well as strong interest in presenting violent or lawless conduct. The play is set at the Big Lake, near Verdigree (Verdigris) Switch, Indian Territory, in 1906. Big Lake, located about thirteen miles southwest of Claremore, is a natural body of water over which Cherokees and Osages quarreled. The Department of the Interior resolved the dispute by declaring the area government property and in the 1920s put the Big Lake district up for sale, after which it was privately developed as a gated community. The Binghams, who are mentioned in the course of the play, were actual property owners on Big Lake. The activity of bootleggers that is central in the play's plot is also well-founded. Prohibition of intoxicants was required in the Indian Territory and Osage Nation for a period of twenty-one years by the Enabling Act authorizing Oklahoma statehood and was extended to the entire state in response to lobbying by dry groups; bootlegging had already been rampant in the nineteenth century.

The tragedy of *Big Lake* centers on a pair of "very young" schoolmates, Betty and Lloyd, who have fallen in love. They both feel oppressed by their home environments and aspire to escape to freedom. In the symbolic structure of the work, the young couple's sense of captivity and danger is embodied in the woods, and their hopes of liberation are represented by the lake. Their dreams end bitterly when they learn that there is no refuge for them and that the lake is the shining face of death.

Part One ("The Woods") shows Betty and Lloyd in the woods bordering Big Lake. Hoping to admire the dawn together, they have arrived ahead of their classmates, who are to be led there by their teacher, Miss Meredith, for a school outing. Both of them, as if a modern Hansel and Gretel, are afraid of the woods, which Betty calls dark and "waitin'." Lloyd persuades her to go out on the lake with him if they can borrow a boat from a cabin nearby.

The scene shifts to the interior of the cabin. The bootlegger Butch Adams enters quickly and tells his companion Elly that he is being followed by the sheriff. Elly, who assumes that it is moonshining that has got him in trouble, becomes the first of Riggs's characters to praise lawlessness as a creed of freedom from societal oppression: "You ain't done nuthin' wrong. It's jist a law. W'at the hell's a law? W'at's it good fer? Why'n't it agin the law everwhur else to sell whiskey? Them men whur they have their corner saloons all polished up—a-makin' it criminal to sell a man a drink—w'at's right about it? . . . Oh, yes! I know. Pertectin' the Indians! They don't want the Indians to git all lit up like *they* do all the time—ever day, ever night, regular. . . . Hell! Indians! I ain't saw two Indians since I come to Indian Territory."

Butch's problem, though, is much more serious. He is being hunted as the killer of Jim Dory, who had told federal officers at Tulsa about Butch's whiskey dealings. Butch knew that the informer was planning to go to a party at the Binghams and stabbed him to death after ambushing him in the big woods close to a sawmill. Dory did not die immediately, and Butch feared that he would identify him as the assailant. He tried to "finish the job," but someone carried the mortally wounded Dory into a store.

When Lloyd and Betty arrive at the cabin, Butch agrees to lend them his boat. Elly's thoughts are in conflict. She has begun to ponder the feasibility of blaming Butch's crime on Lloyd but is torn by the boy's resemblance to her demented brother who drowned in the Big Lake the month before. After their unexpected guests leave, Elly repents her initial thought of inculpating them for Dory's murder, but Butch takes up the idea in earnest. When the sheriff and his deputies arrive, Butch takes a cue from Elly's family tragedy; he tells the lawmen that the killer is his crazy brother who "runs wild here in the woods."

In Scene 1 of Part Two ("The Lake"), the school picnic is in full swing. The censorious schoolmarm criticizes the girls for letting their dancing partners swing them by the waist instead of by the arms and questions Lloyd and Betty closely about their early arrival. Betty and Lloyd row out onto the lake to escape her scolding.

In the concluding Scene 2 the sheriff, mistaking Lloyd for Butch's fictitious wild brother, shoots him dead from the shore, and Betty drowns herself. Butch, in a sudden change of heart, admits his guilt, Miss Meredith is reduced to tears over the loss of her "poor little ones," and Elly slowly intones a determinist lament: "It's always the way. People *will* go on the lake. Young people. Cain't keep 'em off. 'N' they's alwys accidents. Sometimes it's the lake, sometimes it's the woods—boats leak, guns go off, people air keerless, they's wild animals—sump'n happens, sump'n alwys happens. It cain't be helped."

The murder in *Big Lake* and the two tragic deaths that follow in the play's last scene do not appear to be based on actual incidents, but the circumstances of Butch's crime are true to experience in the Indian Territory toward the end of the nineteenth century. A pertinent example is the triple 1897 murder near Rose, Oklahoma, about fifty miles east of Tulsa. Known as the Saline Courthouse Massacre, this case has many of the ingredients of Riggs's plot: bootlegging activity in the area, murder from ambush, the killing of a would-be informer, and the possibility that the first of the three crimes was staged in a way that would cast suspicion on an innocent man.

Professional criminals also appear in Riggs's 1928 drama *The Domino Parlor* (which was later revised as *Hang on to Love*). In 1928 a man who calls himself Jude Summers has for three years been running the Mission Club, a domino parlor in Blackmore, a blending of the names of two Oklahoma towns, Blackwell and Claremore. In 1916, under the name Jack Carpenter, Jude was involved in a bank robbery in Wilmington, Delaware, in which a cashier was killed. Jude seems to have chosen the perfect hideout, because Blackmore's chief of police, Braden, who winks at the whiskey that the Mission Club illegally mixes with its soft drinks, openly admits that car stealing is more in his law enforcement line than murder.

Jude's past, however, returns to Blackmore in the person of Toni Devereaux, who is the star of a wretched musical revue ("tab show") featuring the "Dizzy Red Hots, Mostly Girls," performing at the Lyric Theatre. Toni inadvertently reveals Jude's identity to Charley Troglin, a brutal gambler who has served a term in the penitentiary for murder. When Troglin arranges to inform Chief Braden of his discovery, Toni shoots the gambler in an alley.

In *A Lantern to See By*, an eruption of violence is closely related to what novelist Henry Roth defined as the central theme of Riggs's plays, "the conflict between the impulses of the individual and the constricting forces about him, whether they be the demands of other individuals or the organized demands of society." In the play, set in a farmhouse near Blackmore, John Harmon, a brutal drunkard, tyrannizes his six sons, reserving the most vicious abuse for nineteen-year-old Jodie, whom he attacked with an iron pinch bar offstage in the first scene. John drives his wife, Thursey, to an early death from overwork as well as from the frequent childbirths that he publicly vaunts as evidence of his potency. Young Annie Marble is hired to take over the domestic chores. Jodie falls in love with her. He is shocked to learn, however, that his father has misappropriated wages due him from a job away from the farm as a teamster and that during his absence from home Annie has become his father's mistress. Jodie vents his accumulated grievances against his father at a confrontation in the farm smokehouse and kills him with the pinch bar that John has thrown at him. Annie is furious with Jodie for cutting off the payments she feels sure that the old man, had he lived, would have made for her sexual favors; she was counting on the cash to finance her joining "Ruby Dawson an' some other girls" in "a house—fer men to come to."

Murder is prominent among the social ills of Oklahoma's Cherokees as depicted in *The Cherokee Night.* The episodes of the work move backward and forward in time, the earliest date being 1895 (Scene 7) and the latest 1931 (Scene 3). Each scene is dominated by the profile of Claremore Mound. The ambiguity of that event in Oklahoma historiography, which alternatively describes it as a "battle" or, more realistically, as "a massacre," is reflected in Scene 1 ("Sixty-seven Arrowheads"), set at the mound in 1915. Three young couples, all part Cherokee, encounter an old man, Talbert, who is digging for arrowheads on the mound as an offering to "all the Cherokees," who he believes have lost their birthright since their victory on the mound and have passed into night because, as a warrior apparition has taught him, they have "sunk already to the white man's way." The young people do not all share the old man's fervor, and a schoolteacher, Viney Jones, remembers the Osage sorrow as well as the Cherokees' past glory: "The killing was godawful. And only one woman of the Osage camp got away. Clumb down yand' side of the Mound, swum the river and was never heard of again." Many of the remaining scenes show that white hostility, and the assimilating Indians' self-hatred, have incited new instances of violence and hostility among the Cherokees. A prostitute, Bee Newcomb, is planted in jail to induce mixed-blood Art Osburn's confession to killing his wife, an older Indian woman, Clara Leahy, with a "leathery old face, them eyes all bloodshot, her stringy hair" (Scene 2); a group of part-Cherokee youths show little sympathy when they discover evidence of a murder among blacks (Scene 4); and Gar Breeden, a young man disillusioned with the Cherokee community, faces torture and death at the hands of a Bible-thumping cult (Scene 5). In Scene 7, set in 1895, a peaceful full-blood Cherokee, Gray-Wolf, witnesses a posse's murder of a half-white outlaw, Edgar Breeden (Gar Breeden's father), who was, says Gray-Wolf, "not enough Indian" to forgo a life of crime. Lawman Tinsley crows to Gray-Wolf, "Tell ever'body what it means to oppose the law. You Indians must think you own things out here. This is God's country out here—and God's a white man. Don't forget that."

Two plays by Lynn Riggs, both thematically related to *Green Grow the Lilacs,* treat crime and rebelliousness in a comic spirit. In the one-act *Knives from Syria,* produced by the Santa Fe Players in 1925, a Syrian peddler is able to run off with a farm girl, Rhodie, because the hired man,

Charley, who woos her with her widowed mother's blessing, believes that he is pursued by killers. Actually, Charley is the victim of a prank. *Roadside* (1930)—expanded from an original one-act version, *Reckless*—features a high-spirited cowboy yarn spinner named Texas (played by Ralph Bellamy in the 1930 New York run) who, when arraigned for intoxication, kicked the judge off the bench, made a hash of the courthouse, and breaks out of jail. Unlike Curly, who is domesticated by Laurey at the end of *Green Grow the Lilacs,* Texas chooses a life on the move with the spunky teenager who has won his heart, Hannie. In a program for the 1941 production at Baylor University, Riggs described *Roadside* as "a comedy about the impossible dream man has always had: complete freedom, the right to be lawless, uncircumspect, gusty and hearty, anarchic, fun loving, chicken stealing if necessary (for where there is no ordinary morality, there is of course no crime)."

The Quest for "Pore Jud"

Lynn Riggs completed *Green Grow the Lilacs* in 1929 during a stay in France financed by a grant from the Guggenheim Foundation. The play is set near Claremore in 1900, seven years before Oklahoma's admission to the Union. Riggs included nineteenth-century songs and ballads in the work, intending "solely to recapture in a kind of nostalgic glow (but in dramatic dialogue more than in song) the great range of mood which characterized the old folk songs and ballads I used to hear in my Oklahoma childhood—their quaintness, their sadness, their robustness, their simplicity, their hearty or bawdy humors, their sentimentalities, their melodrama, their touching sweetness."

On November 27, 1947, Riggs answered an inquiry of Marion Starr Mumford of Claremore about the biographical origins of his characters in *Green Grow the Lilacs.* He responded: "Aunt Eller is based on my wonderful Aunt Mary—(Mrs. John Brice)—and some of the things I vaguely knew about my mother—who died when I was two—(Her name, too, was Ella. "Eller," as people called her). . . . Laurey was my cousin Laura Thompson, who died some time ago. She was glowing and lovely—and made a deep and tender and lasting impression on me. Curly was a cowboy who used to work for my aunt." The letter is silent about the real-life basis of the play's villain, Jeeter Fry, but Riggs's relatives and friends have identified him as a farmhand named Jetar (sometimes misspelled Jeeter) Davis. Only occasionally is Davis remembered as sharing any of Jeeter Fry's repellent traits. Biographer Phyllis Cole Braunlich writes that "Jeeter, in fact, was known as one of the meanest boys in town." An article in the *Rogers County Historical Society Newsletter* of March/May 1999 asserts that Jeeter Fry was in reality "a man named Jeeter Davis who pulled a knife on a family member."

In 1998 Howard McNeill gave the *Chanute* (Kansas) *Tribune*'s managing editor Stu Butcher a far less disturbing version of Davis's character: "His name was Jeeter Davis and I remember him just like it was yesterday. He was a farmhand, but one of these guys who would get drunk on Saturday and thought he was a whiz with the women and . . . he was just a dirty old boy." By far the greatest repository of knowledge of Jetar Davis (including the correct spelling of his first name) lay in the prodigious memory of Lynn Riggs's nephew, Leo Cundiff, who responded by email on April 1, 2002, to my inquiry about Davis. "All that I have heard about [Jetar] Davis was that he was sort of the town drunk," Cundiff wrote. "Several of the townspeople would make fun of him and play jokes on him. I am told that he was not a threat to anyone except himself. He used to carry mortar for a brick mason and when a carnival would come to town, he would oblige one of their performers by wrestling with him. I am told he was pretty good."

Cundiff was able to supply other biographical details about Jetar Davis that may be crucial to understanding Davis's transformation into Riggs's Jeeter Fry and later into Jud Fry ("Pore Jud") in *Oklahoma!* Jetar was a close contemporary of Lynn Riggs; he was born in Claremore on August 9, 1899 (a few weeks before Riggs), and died in 1958. Moreover, like Riggs, Jetar had Cherokee blood.

In Scene 1 of *Green Grow the Lilacs,* Curly McClain refers to Jeeter Fry, the hired hand on Laurey Williams's farm, as "that bullet-colored growly man 'th the bushy eyebrows," and the introductory stage directions of Scene 3, set in the farm's smokehouse, describe Jeeter as having "a curious earth-colored face and hairy hands." Without the benefit of Leo Cundiff's biographical revelations, Roger Aikin intuitively reaches a sound conclusion that knowledge of the real-life Jetar Davis fortifies: Jeeter Fry is the cowboy hero Curly's "dark side." From this promising beginning of his argument, however, Aikin proceeds to a dubious conclusion, that Fry can be best understood as the son of parents who "came from the wrong part of Europe, perhaps in that great immigrant wave after 1880." It is more plausible that the character of Jeeter Fry, and his dark color, reflect

Jetar Davis, on whom Jud Fry is said to be based. Pencil drawing by forensic artist Linda Spurlock after a photographic image furnished by Leo and Gary Cundiff.

the Cherokee in Lynn Riggs and the dramatist's painful sense of the devaluation of Cherokees in American life.

In *Green Grow the Lilacs,* Jeeter Fry's low self-esteem accounts for much of his unlovely conduct that makes his young employer, Laurey Williams, afraid of him, although he is essential to the operation of her farm. In Scene 2 Laurey tells Aunt Eller that she hooks her door at night and fastens her windows because she hears the sound of feet walking around the corner of the house and in the front room and wakes to hear boards creaking. Fry holes up in the smokehouse, feeding his sexual fantasies on pink covers from the *Police Gazette* and pornographic postcards that he buys from a peddler. Laurey feels constrained to accept his invitation to an evening of square dances, songs, and games ("play-party"), but when he makes unwanted advances to her outside their host's house, she fires him. He accuses her of regarding herself as "so goddamned much better" and threatens revenge.

Fry's menaces terrify Laurey because she is obsessed with the dangers of fire and arson. In Scene 2, when she had confided her fears of Jeeter to her aunt, she told Eller that as a child she had seen a farmhouse ablaze as she rode in a covered wagon with her parents on her way to Claremore. The farmer's wife sat at the roadside and lamented, "Now my home's burnt up. 'F I'd jist a-give him a piece of cold pork or sump'n. If I'd jist a-fed him!" The young Laurey had understood the woman to blame a resentful itinerant for setting the fire, and this traumatic memory led her to worry persistently about the risk that Jeeter would torch the Williams farm. This concern was stirred to panic by Jeeter's angry words after his discharge.

The violent resolution of the play's amorous triangle in Scene 5 demonstrates that, despite the effort of Aunt Eller to calm her fears, Laurey was right to be nervous. After her wedding to Curly, Jeeter Fry attempts to torch the haystack that the newlyweds are forced to mount by their boisterous neighbors. The couple is saved, and Fry is killed during a scuffle with Curly when he falls on his own knife.

Jeeter Fry's murderous designs against Laurey and her cowboy had been far from unprecedented. When in Scene 3 Curly McClain pays a visit to Fry in his smokehouse lair, he learns more about the farmhand than even Laurey suspects in her recurrent premonitions: he is a serial murderer. Riggs's study of Jeeter's large-scale homicidal mania is eerily predictive of a phenomenon of which most Americans were only dimly aware before 1966, when Charles Whitman's sniper shots from a tower on the campus of the University of Texas killed fifteen and wounded thirty random victims. Curly shows considerable detective-like skill in worming a veiled confession from the reclusive, fantasy-ridden Jeeter, who resents employers and others he believes regard themselves as his "betters." His tongue loosened by Curly's singing of the hanging ballad of Sam Hall, Jeeter (who shares the compulsion of many serial killers to avow or describe their crimes) narrates two separate outrages that he attributes to unnamed murderers:

A farm girl's suitor came upon her in the barn loft with another man. One morning her father found his daughter in a horse trough, "in her nightgown, layin' there in the water all covered with blood, dead." The killer probably threw her in the trough because "he couldn't stand havin' blood on him."

A married farmer was carrying on a passionate affair with a girl. When she told him that she was pregnant, he bound her hands and feet, threw her on top of a haystack and set fire to it. "He didn't keer about her goin' to have the baby, that wasn't it. He jist didn't know how he was goin' to live 'thout *havin'* her all the time while she was carryin' it. So he killed her."

Even these two killings do not necessarily exhaust Fry's catalog of horror. He also tells Curly of previous employers near Quapaw, and before that near Tulsa, who were "bastards to work fer, both of 'em, . . . always makin' out they were *better*." Curly, alerted by Jeeter's murder narratives, asks whether he had got even, but the hired man abruptly breaks off his disclosures. It is too late for silence, though. Curly has already heard enough for his cowboy heart to despise the hired hand as a "festering" loner hiding from the sunlight: "In this country, they's two things you c'n do if you're a man. Live out of doors is one. Live in a hole is the other. I've set by my horse in the bresh some'eres and heared a rattlesnake many a time. Rattle, rattle, rattle!—he'd go, skeered to death. Skeered and *dangerous!* Somebody comin' close to his hole! Somebody gonna step on him! Git his old fangs ready, full of pizen!"

In the smokehouse scene in *Oklahoma!* (Act One, Scene 2), Oscar Hammerstein conflated the two murders that Jeeter Fry indirectly acknowledges in Riggs's play. In Hammerstein's version, Jud Fry tells of a hired hand who, after finding his sweetheart on the Bartlett farm in the hayloft with a rival, bought a supply of kerosene over a period of weeks and burned down the farmhouse, killing the girl and both her parents. When he is left alone at the scene's end, Jud, who had earlier joined in Curly's comic threnody "Pore Jud is Daid," delivers a solo of a darker hue, "Lonely Room." This monologue of revenge and sexual longing (generally underappreciated before Shuler Hensley's strong performance in the Trevor Nunn revival) begins by invoking Jud's solitude:

The floor creaks,
The door squeaks,
There's a fieldmouse a-nibblin' on a broom,
And I set by myself
Like a cobweb on a shelf,
By myself in a lonely room.

In the song's middle section, Jud's erotic musing about the "soft arms" and "long, yeller hair" of his dream girl follows his burst of anger against Curly: "And I'm better'n that Smart Alec cowhand / Who thinks he is better'n me!" The chilling finale of the song vows that Jud will translate his lustful fantasies into action: "I ain't gonna dream 'bout her arms no more! / I ain't gonna leave her alone!"

When Lynn Riggs attended a rehearsal of *Oklahoma!* for the first time, Oscar Hammerstein asked whether he approved of "Lonely Room." The playwright replied, "I certainly do. It will scare hell out of the audience." Hammerstein was pleased: "That is exactly what it was designed to do."

Hammerstein invented another plot element that lends further emphasis to Jud Fry's homicidal fixation on Curly: a cylindrical peephole toy, called "the Little Wonder," that is secretly fitted with a spring-blade knife. Only Aunt Eller's timely intervention prevents Jud from attacking Curly with the insidious weapon at the box social.

Jeeter Fry is not the only source of violence in *Green Grow the Lilacs*. Communal disorder is institutionalized through the use of the "shivaree," a noisy mock-serenade or sometimes more aggressive hazing of newly-weds that leaves its modern traces in the tin cans tied to the rear bumper of the bridal couple's honeymoon car. It was the shivaree that encouraged Jeeter to imitate his earlier murder of the pregnant girl: the mob of neighbors taunting the newlyweds forced them onto the haystack that Jeeter tried to set afire. When Jeeter is killed during his fight with Curly after the fire is extinguished, the neighbors urge Curly to give himself up to authorities, even though Jeeter had accidentally fallen on his own knife. Aunt Eller tells Laurey (in Scene 6) that the male community has surrendered Curly not to uphold the law but to preserve the disreputable custom of shivareeing, which had facilitated Fry's assault: "But you know the way everybody feels about shivoreein'. They got a right to it somehow. And a thing like this a-happenin' in the middle of a shivoree—why, it looks *bad,* that's all." As the curtain falls on *Green Grow the Lilacs,* there is every expectation that shivarees will continue and that Curly will be freed after facing trial. *Oklahoma!*'s finale speeds Curly's liberation by convening a kangaroo court to acquit him on the spot. Some theatergoers deride this happy finale as make-believe, but the lightninglike deliverance of Bessie Thompson by her Sapulpa jury should remind us not to underrate the nimbleness of early-twentieth-century Oklahoma justice.

Aunt Eller's Sermon

When Laurey, in the final scene of *Green Grow the Lilacs,* despairs over the jailing of Curly, Aunt Eller preaches a sermon of survival, saying, "Oh, lots of things happens to a womern. Sickness, bein' pore and hungry even, bein' left alone in yer old age, bein' afraid to die—it all adds up. That's the way life is—cradle to grave. And you c'n stand it. They's one way. You got to be hearty. You *got* to be." Aunt Eller's creed of "heartiness" is not founded on an optimism born of innocence, for she too has experienced the Oklahoma violence that infuses Lynn Riggs's memories and writings. Eller is not a spinster, as many of her comic portrayals in Rodgers and Hammerstein's musical may have led audiences to believe, but a widow whose husband, Jack Murphy, was murdered. Jack had "bought some hogs off Lem Slocum, and they turned out to be full of cholery—and all died." Jack walked across the pasture to complain to his seller, and then night fell. When Eller went searching for him, she found his body near a worm fence, all huddled down in a corner—"Laid there all doubled up—dead—in a patch of yeller daisies. Len Slocum musta shot him. I didn't know *who* done it. All I knowed was—*my husband was dead.*" To Eller, the identity of the murderer and the rights and wrongs of the quarrel that took her husband from her were secondary concerns that lost themselves in life's fragility and the immutable fact of loss. With her homely eloquence she beautifully expresses the lesson of Lynn Riggs's plays.

Bibliographical Notes

The plays of Lynn Riggs cited in this article are: *Big Lake* (New York: Samuel French, 1927), 15, 81; *The Cherokee Night,* in Russet Mantle *and* The Cherokee Night (New York: Samuel French, 1936), 139, 197, 260; *Cream in the Well,* in *Four Plays* (New York: Samuel French, 1947); *Dark Encounter,* in *Four Plays; Green Grow the Lilacs* (New York: Samuel French, 1931), vii, 19, 69–71, 75, 91, 143, 145–46; *Hang on to Love* (New York: Samuel French, 1948 [a revision of *The Domino Parlor*]), 21–23, 28, 131; *Knives from Syria,* in *One-Act Plays for Stage and Study,* 3rd ser. (New York: Samuel French, 1927); *A Lantern to See By,* in Sump'n Like Wings *and* A Lantern to See By (New York: Samuel French, 1928); *Roadside* (New York: Samuel French, 1930); *Russet Mantle,* in Russet Mantle *and* The Cherokee Night; *A World Elsewhere,* in *Four Plays; The Year of Pilár,* in *Four Plays.*

The successive drafts of Riggs's unfinished novel "The Affair at Easter" in its unfinished state and a related working notebook and other papers are deposited in the Lynn Riggs Papers (YCAL MSS 61, box 9, folder 173 to box 10, folder 184) at the Beinecke Rare Book and Manuscript Library, Yale University Library, New Haven, Connecticut.

My account of the Sapulpa, Oklahoma, murder case, on which Riggs's novel is partially based, draws on the reports in the *Sapulpa Herald,* which were furnished to me by the courteous staff of the Sapulpa Historical Society.

The principal biography of Lynn Riggs is Phyllis Cole Braunlich's *Haunted by Home: The Life and Letters of Lynn Riggs* (Norman: Univ. of Oklahoma Press, 1988), 21–24, 64–65, 170–71. I am also indebted to Mrs. Braunlich for insights she generously provided in our telephone conversations. I also consulted Charles Edward Aughtry, "Lynn Riggs, Dramatist: A Critical Biography" (Ph.D. diss., Brown University, 1959), 143.

Oscar Hammerstein's praise of *Green Grows the Lilacs* appeared in his letter to the "Drama Mailbag" of the *New York Times,* Sept. 5, 1943.

Lynn Riggs's sense of "hidden excitement" in Oklahoma is quoted from his "When People Say 'Folk Drama,'" *The Carolina Play-Book* 4 (June 1931).

U.S. Marshal Evett Dumas Nix's comment on the Doolin gang is quoted in his *Oklahombres,* as told to Gordon Hines (St. Louis: Eden Publishing House, 1929), 56.

Ronald Trekel's observation that the Doolins "never plundered or killed in Tulsa" is found in Ronald L. Trekel, *History of the Tulsa Police Department* (Topeka, Kans.: Jostens Corporation, 1989), 19.

Rufus Buck's spree is detailed in Carl Sifakis, *The Encyclopedia of American Crime* (New York: Facts on File, 1982), 217–18.

The quote from the unfinished Gerard Manley Hopkins poem in Riggs's draft of "The Affair at Easter" is found in W. H. Gardner and N. H. MacKenzie, eds., *The Poems of Gerald Manley Hopkins,* 4th ed. (London: Oxford Univ. Press, 1967), 193.

168 · *Musical Mysteries*

The Claremore massacre is described in *"Claremore's Historical Summary,"* http://www.claremore.org/historicalsociety/history.htm (accessed March 29, 2002; site now discontinued).

The Guthrie "racial outbreak" is noted in Arrell Morgan Gibson, *Oklahoma: A History of Five Centuries,* 2nd ed. (Norman: Univ. of Oklahoma Press, 1981), 213.

Professor Thomas Erhard's argument that *Hang on to Love* reflects Riggs's horror of lynchings is in Erhard's *Lynn Riggs, Southwest Playwright* (Austin, Tex.: Steck-Vaughn, 1970), 37.

Henry Roth's definition of Riggs's theme as a conflict of individual impulses and constricting social forces found in Henry Roth, "Lynn Riggs and the Individual" [1930], in *Shifting Landscapes: A Composite, 1925–1987,* ed. Mario Materassi (Philadelphia: Jewish Publication Society, 1987), 13.

Professor Roger C. Aikin identifies Jud Fry as Jewish in his article "Property, Race, and Gender in "Oklahoma!" http://puffin-creighton.edu/fapa/aikin/Web-files/WEST/property.htm (accessed Feb. 5, 2002; site now discontinued).

Oscar Hammerstein's intention to frighten audiences with the song "Lonely Room" is quoted in Max Wilk, *OK! The Story of Oklahoma!* (New York: Grove Press, 1993), 83–84.

In telephone conversations I was fortunate in obtaining recollections of Riggs's first cousin (once removed), Howard McNeill, on a fire that may have inspired a similar near-catastrophe at the end of those works. His daughter, Melinda McNeill, has enlightened me on details of the Riggs-Thompson genealogy. Leo Cundiff, nephew of Lynn Riggs and long the keeper of his uncle's memory, was very instructive to me about his family and its Oklahoma roots. He was able to tell me much about Jetar Davis, the part-Cherokee hod carrier, amateur wrestler, and "sort of the town drunk" who was immortalized as Jud Fry in *Oklahoma!*

Index

Bernard, Christopher, 82–84
Bernstein, Leonard, 95–96
Betty (in *Big Lake*), 156–57
The Biblical Antiquities of Philo (Pseudo-Philo), 110–11
Big Lake (Riggs), 155–58
Bigamy, 107, 117–18
Blankenship, Jessica, 99–100
Blitzstein, Marc, xi; convictions of killers, 90–91; death in Capote's "Music for Chameleons," 94–95; death of, 89, 90–94; works of, 87–90, 96
Blitzstein Strikes Back (Ellis), 97
Blom, Eric, 28, 36
Bloom, Richard, 103
Boelza (or Belza), Igor, 28–29, 36
Bonnet, Jacques, 65, 69
The Book of Moses (Smith), 114–15
Borromeo, Carlo, 51, 56
Borzelli, Angelo, 63
Bourdelot, Pierre, 65, 69
Bourgeois, Louis, 39, 44, 46–47
Brantley, Ben, 143
Brantôme, Abbé (Pierre de Bourdeilles), 58, 64
Braunlich, Phyllis Cole, 161
Breitman, Michel, 64
Brifaut, Charles, 118–20
Bubble Act (1720), 131
Buck, Rufus, 145
"The burial question," Mozart's, 29
Butcher, Stu, 161

Caedmon, 116
Cain: crimes and punishment of descendants and, 109–13, 115; curse of descendants and, 116, 121; forgiveness and reconciliation of descendants and, 121–23; in *Lamech, ou Les Descendants de Caïn*, 118–20; Lamech and, 107–9, 117; Lamech killing, 111, *112*, 116–17
Cain (Blitzstein), 87
Cambert, Robert, x; death of, 3, 8, 11, 13; lack of death and burial records for, 11–13; Lully and, 3, 9–10; Perrin and, 4–6; reception in England, 7, 10–11, 13; talent of, 4–5, 14
Capote, Truman, 94–95

Carafa, Fabrizio (Duke of Andria): Consiglio's portrayal of, 60–61; investigation into murder of, 53–55; murder in sonnets, drama, and stories, 57–61; murder of, xi, 54–55; murdered body of, 52–53, 61; possible son of, 56
Carafa, Federigo, 51
"Carlo Gesualdo Considered as a Murderer" (Gray), 61–62
Carp, Louis, 21
Carpani, Giuseppe, 26
Carte, Richard D'Oyly, 126, *132, 137*
Casey, Bert, 145
The Catcher in the Rye, Chapman's obsession with, 99–100, 102–3
Caulfield, Holden (in *Catcher in the Rye*), 99–100
Chapman, Gloria Abe, 98, 101
Chapman, Mark David: background of, 98–100; desire for fame, 103–4; Lennon killed by, xi–xii, 102; mental state of, 99–100, 103; mixed feelings about Lennon, 100, 102–3; obsession with *Catcher in the Rye*, 99–100, 102–3; plan to murder Lennon, 101–2
Charles, Jacques-Pierre, 41, 45
Charles II, and Cambert, 7–8
Chaucer, Geoffrey, 117–18
The Cherokee Night (Riggs), 155, 159
Chigi, Flavio, 66–67
Claremore, Oklahoma, 153–55, 159–60
Claremore Mound Massacre, 153, 159
Clark, Kenneth, 19
Claude, Antoine, 43
Closset, Nikolaus, 18, 26
Clough, Arthur Hugh, 121–23
Companies Act of 1862, Gilbert satirizing, 125, 131, 133, 135–36
Composers: conspiracy against, 80–82; operatic, 4; vulnerability of freelancing, 66. See also *specific individuals*
The Condemned (Blitzstein), 87
Consiglio, Alberto, 60–61
Contarini, Alvise, 67–69
Corona Manuscript, 51–53, 59, 63
Corporations: British legislation governing, 125, 131; Gilbert's interest in business law and, 128–29, 136–37; in Gilbert's plays, 129–30, 132–38,